# HarpART

GREAT PORTRAITS
the artists, the musicians
& their instruments

by Tim Stuart

Published in 2007 by
We Do Music
Mold
Wales

www.wedomusic.co.uk



ISBN 978 0 9556108 0 6



Designed and printed in the United Kingdom.

# FOREWORD

This is a book of portraits, great portraits for the most part. Some of them are well known, others much less so, but it is hoped that they will all delight the eye of the viewer.

*A book for all harpists and lovers of portraiture.*

## Images and Citations

The author is grateful to the curators of the museums, art galleries and image libraries for supplying the images and, where they are copyright holders, granting permission for their reproduction.

**Introduction** Unknown sculptor *Harpist* from Cyclades islands, Greece, 3rd millennium BC, National Archaeological Museum, Athens © Photo SCALA Florence 1990. Unknown artist *Musicians and a Dancer* from the Tomb of Nakht, New Kingdom, late 2nd millennium BC (wall painting), The Bridgeman Art Library. Unknown artist *Fragment with Apollo* Palatine Antiquarium Museum, Rome, courtesy of the Ministero Beni e Att. Culturali © Photo SCALA Florence 1990. Grassi, Giovannino de' (c1350–1398) *Page from Sketchbook with girls playing musical instruments* late C14, Biblioteca Civica 'Angelo Mai', Bergamo © Photo SCALA Florence 1990. Unknown artist, The Westminster Psalter *King David as psalmist* c1200 ©The British Library Board. All rights reserved, Royal 2 A. XXII. Bosch, Hieronymus, 1450–1516, detail of *Garden of Earthly Delights* 1504, Museo del Prado © Prado, Madrid, Spain/ The Bridgeman Art Library. Zampieri, Domenichino 1581–1641, *King David with a harp* early C17 © Photo RMN – Daniel Arnaudet, Musée national du château et de Trianon, Versailles
**Holbein, Hans** 1498–1543 (circle of) *Xylotectus (Johannes Zimmermann)* 1520 Photo reproduced by kind permission of the Germanisches Nationalmuseum, Nuremberg. *The Ambassadors / Portrait of Jean de Dinteville and Georges de Selve* by Hans Holbein the younger with detail of lute, 1533, Photo © Trustees of the National Gallery, London
**Lanfranco, Giovanni** c1582–1647 *La Musica (Venere che suona l'arpa)* c1632 Galleria Nazionale d'Arte Antica, Rome, Photo © Archivio Fotografico Soprintendenza Speciale per il Polo Museale Romano. Barberini Harp in the Museo Nazionale degli Strumenti Musicali, Rome, Photo © Archivio Fotografico Soprintendenza Speciale
**Nuvolone, Carlo Francesco** 1608–c1661 *The Artist's Family* c1662 Pinacoteca di Brera, Milan © Photo SCALA Florence 1990
**Hogarth, William** 1697–1764 *David Lewis* c1732 courtesy of Aberdeen Art Gallery & Museums Collections. *The Rose Tavern* (No 3 of *The Rake's Progress*) 1735, C19th engraving, after original painting in Sir John Soane Museum, London
**Greuze, Jean-Baptiste** 1727–1805 *Ange-Laurent de Lalive de Jully* c1759 Samuel H Kress collection, image © 2007, Board of Trustees, National Gallery of Art, Washington. *Wolfgang Amadeus Mozart* 1763–64, Yale University Collection of Musical Instruments, New Haven
**Reynolds, Sir Joshua** 1723-1792 *The Countess of Eglinton* 1777 ©Private Collection Agnew's, London, UK/The Bridgeman Art Library
**Gainsborough, Thomas** 1727-1788 *Louisa, Lady Clarges* 1778 courtesy of the Holburne Museum of Art, Bath. *Portrait of Johann Christian Bach*, 1776, Museo Bibliografico Musicale, Bologna © Photo SCALA Florence 1990
**Giroust, Jean Antoine** 1753–1817 *Madame de Genlis et les enfants du duc d'Orléans: La leçon de harpe donnée au château de Saint-Leu en présence de mademoiselle Pamela* c1790 [copy by Mauzaisse, Jean-Baptiste, 1784–1844 c1843] © Photo RMN – Hervé Lewandowski, Musée national du château et de Trianon. Cosway, Richard 1742–1821 *Young Louis Philippe, the Duke of Montpensier, the Count of Beaujolais and Madame Adélaïde* c1786 © Photo RMN – René-Gabriel Ojéda, Musée Condé, Chantilly
**Ducreux, Rose-Adélaïde** 1761–1802 *Self-portrait with a harp* c1790 courtesy of the Metropolitan Museum of Art, New York, bequest of Susan Dwight Bliss, 1966, 67.55.1, Photo © 1983, Metropolitan Museum of Art. Mallet, Jean Baptiste 1759–1835 *Meeting in a Salon* 1790 ©Musée Marmottan, Paris, France/The Bridgeman Art Library. Vestier, Antoine 1740–1824 *Portrait d'une jeune harpiste* 1805, Cl. J.–P. Elie. Musées de Sens, France
**Ibbetson, Julius Caesar** 1759–1817 *Peasants singing with blind harpist John Smith / Peasants of Caernarvonshire near Conway singing penillion to the harp of John Smith the celebrated blind harper of Conway* 1792 courtesy of National Museums & Galleries of Wales, Cardiff. *Conway Castle* 1794, Victoria & Albert Museum, London
**Sully, Thomas** 1783–1872 *Lady with a harp; Eliza Ridgely* 1818 gift of Maude Monell Vetlesen, image © 2007, Board of Trustees, National Gallery of Art, Washington. *Queen Victoria* 1838 © By kind permission of the Trustees of the Wallace Collection, London
**Raeburn, Sir Henry** 1756–1823 c1820 *The Marchioness of Northampton, Playing a Harp* ©Private Collection/The Bridgeman Art Library. *Rev Robert Walker Skating on Duddingston Loch* 1784, National Gallery of Scotland, Edinburgh
**Lawrence, Sir Thomas** 1769–1830 *Lady Elizabeth Conyngham* 1822 Photo courtesy of Museu Calouste Gulbenkian, Lisbon. *George IV* 1822, © By kind permission of the Trustees of the Wallace Collection, London. *Dital Harp by Egan & Sons* Dublin c1820, courtesy of the Museo dell'Arpa Victor Salvi, Piasco, Italy, Photographer P. Dell'Aquila
**David, Jacques-Louis** 1748-1825 *Juliette de Villeneuve* 1824 © Photo RMN – Jean-Gilles Berizzi, Musée du Louvre, Paris
**Postscript:** Kilburne, George 1839–1924 *The harp lesson* c1900 Private Collection. Photographer Steve Rawlins

# Contents

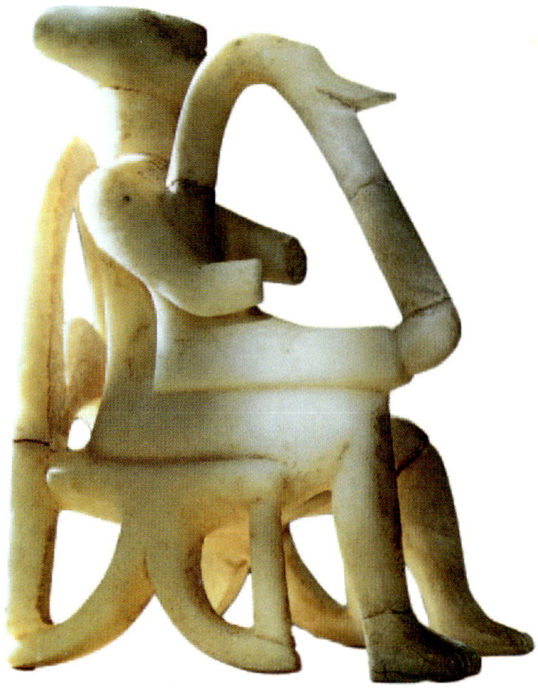

# Introduction
## The first 4000 years

Take a look at the image above. Is it a twentieth-century sculpture? Perhaps it's by Modigliani or Henry Moore. In fact this beautiful image of a seated harpist 'in action' was carved out of marble on one of the Cycladean islands in the Aegean around 4,500 years ago. Now let's get this right: the artefact is nothing at all to do with Greek classical civilization (which didn't develop for another thousand years). It's from the Bronze Age. The Cycladean musician would have been playing on his harp (none of the harpists so far discovered have been identifiably female) around the time that the early inhabitants of Wiltshire were erecting the bluestones of Stonehenge and the builders of Giza topping out their great pyramid.

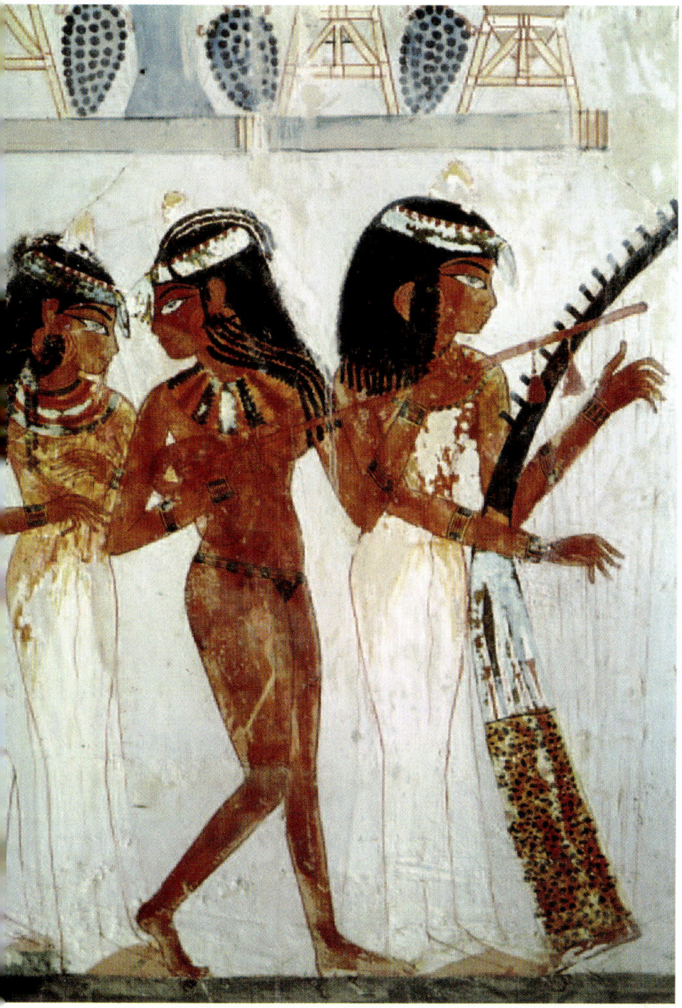

*Musicians and a Dancer*
Tomb of Nakht, Egypt, (New Kingdom) late 2nd millennium BC

Sadly, nothing is known about the musical culture of that time, because no music or written documents from the era have been discovered. But it would be a good guess that harpists were important people. Not only did they sit on chairs (rather rare in the Bronze Age), they were also uniquely commemorated in stone. Perhaps they were transmitters of folklore or religious messages through playing and singing. Maybe they fulfilled the role of priests or soothsayers. We don't know.

Neither do we know anything about the actual music the harpists played. Several pieces of classical Greek music have now been deciphered with some certainty, but it would be wrong to assume that this music had any relationship with the Bronze Age as few direct links with the earlier Aegean culture have been identified.

Although there are plenty of illustrations of plucked string instruments from the civilisations of Egypt and Assyria, most of the instruments that resemble harps from that era were of the 'open' or pillarless variety, rather different from the instruments that we now think of as harps. Some actual string instruments have survived from ancient times — a few complete ones from Egyptian tombs — so we know that the illustrations are similar to the actual instruments themselves, and from the relics we have some idea what they sounded like.

But we do not have many pictures of harps from the more recent classical cultures of Greece or Rome. Greek and Roman musicians played the *lyre* more frequently — or at least the men did. It is possible that harps were more numerous and were played by women, but we have few illustrations because women played a much less well-recorded role in the culture.

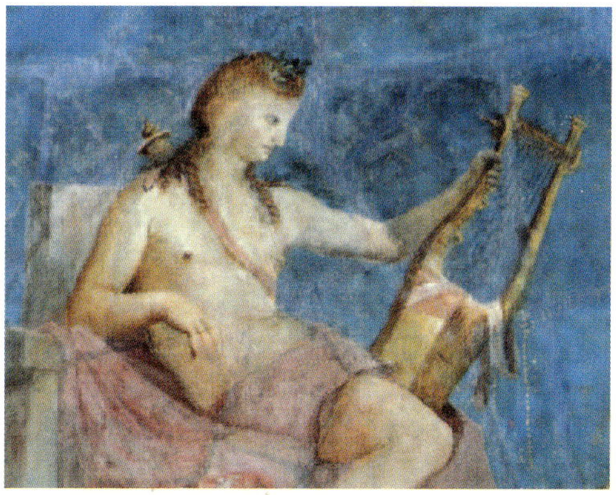

*Apollo with his Lyre*
Roman Wall Painting

Following the demise of classical civilizations, the harp then more or less entirely disappears from European view for over 500 years. When it reappears in medieval art of the ninth century,[1] it is somewhat closer in design to the harp we know today than its Cycladean prototype, although some instruments still appear to lack a fore-pillar. Unlike most of the ancient harps these are small enough to be easily carried.

Progressively illustrations showed changes such as a rounded neck and a gradual trend towards larger instruments, including a more developed sound box. It seems that the full 'harmonic curve' characteristic of harps and other modern multi-stringed instruments developed only slowly. The first instrument to appear in something close to a modern form was the Irish harp of the fourteenth century, although earlier images, such as that of King David from the Westminster Psalter of about 1200 show harps with very recognisable features.

One of the most delightful images of the harp from the medieval era is by Giovannino de' Grassi. This fourteenth-century artist is known as the illustrator of a 'Model Book' which includes realistic scenes of everyday life, and also as the architect of Milan Cathedral.

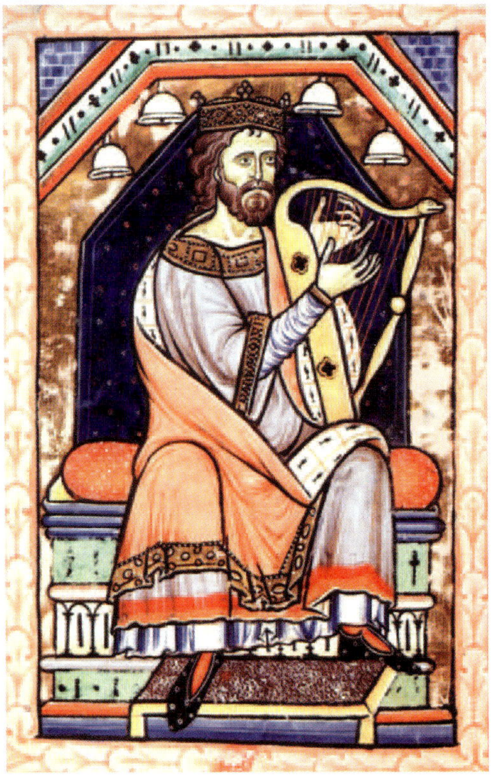

*King David as Psalmist*
Westminster Psalter, C1200

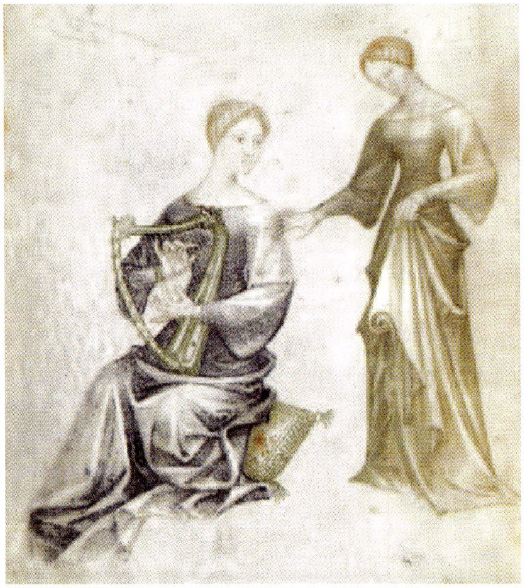

Page from *Sketchbook*
Giovannino de' Grassi, late C14

But in Europe, most art from the medieval era that has survived was sacred: its purpose was to assist in the explanation of biblical stories to an illiterate population. Since the word 'harp' appears some 56 times in the Bible, there was ample scope for illustrations of the instrument and the early artists took full advantage of that. Ironically, the original Hebrew texts referred to the instrument as a *kinnor*, and there seems to be a modern consensus that this was actually a strummed instrument like a lyre or zither. No matter, the medieval artists interpreted the instrument as a harp, and that was what was drawn — and in large numbers.

Frequently the illustrations are in association with King David, many in 'psalteries', which were illustrated books with the text of the psalms.

Apart from King David, the other main performers on the harp in Christian religious art are angels. Exactly how this association arose is not clear, as there is no direct biblical reference to such an angelic accomplishment.

Although many medieval and renaissance examples of heavenly harpists are to be found, and there is representation in the corpus of art by Dürer, Van Eyck, Fra Angelico, Roubiliac and others, the intimate association between the harp, angels and heaven appears to have been particularly fostered as a romantic ideal in the nineteenth century.[2] The other religious personality sometimes associated with the harp is St Cecilia, the patron saint of musicians. Although images of her playing the harp do occur,[3] and Reynolds may allude to her in his portrait in this book, she is more likely to be seen playing the organ.

But one must not forget non-Christian religions. The Roman goddess of love, Venus, can be observed playing the harp in Lanfranco's picture, reproduced below.

Not all representations of the harp are in a benign context. Sirens, a particularly nasty variety of mermaid, would sometimes lure seamen to their deaths by twanging their harps. Hieronymus Bosch's sadistic depictions of the harp in the underworld as an instrument of torture must also be mentioned.

Thus, for one reason or another, the illustration of the harp in historical and allegorical art came to be a relatively frequent occurrence. Besides the artists so far mentioned one must also record Memling, Lastmann, Rubens and Rembrant, and the instrument that was pictured was usually a contemporary one. Such were the associations between musicians and artists that it is likely that an actual harp would have been on hand to form the basis of their illustrations. In consequence, they would be an important source of information about the instruments of the artists' time and place.[4]

But this book is concerned with *portraits*, not sacred, historical or allegorical paintings. The definition generally followed here is that of a picture in which the artist, for whatever reason, is *making a statement about a particular individual*, not using him or her as a proxy for a historical or mythological figure whose true likeness was unknown.

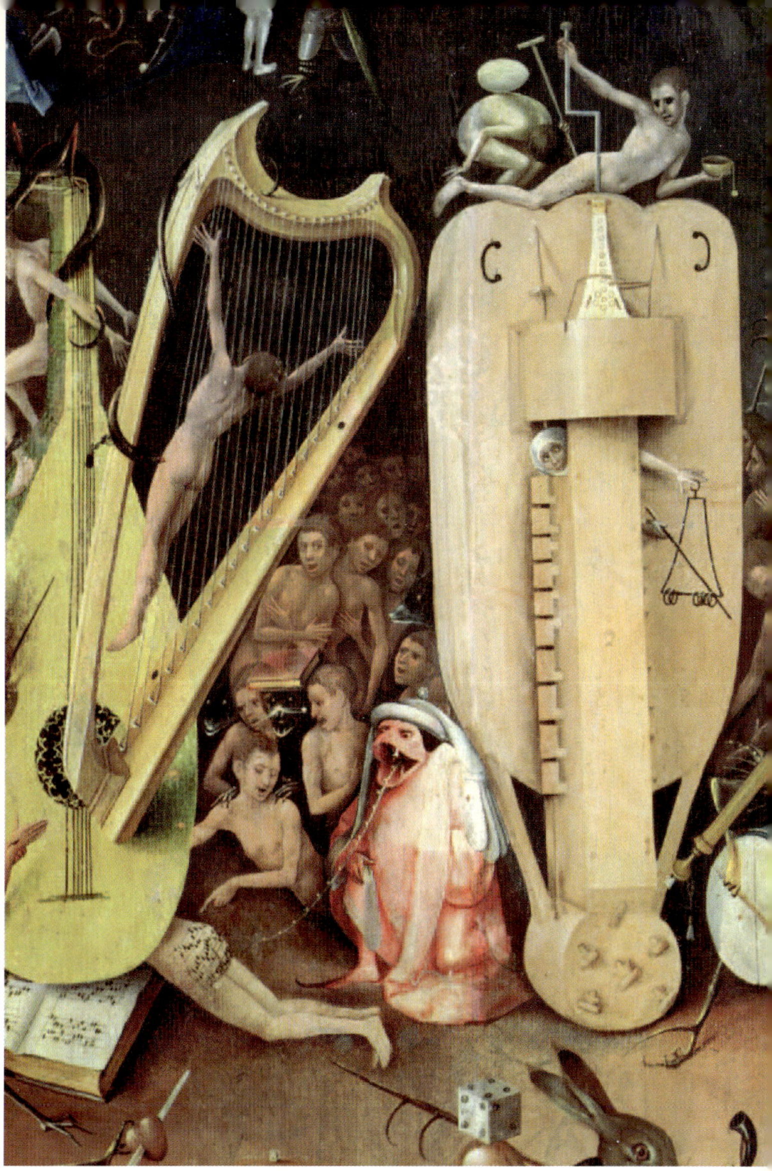

Detail from *Garden of Earthly Delights*
H Bosch, 1504

Of course, the distinctions can be blurred.

On the one hand, an artist might use a known sitter to pose in his historical or allegorical scene.[5]

On the other hand, a portraitist might choose an artificial historical or allegorical context for a portrait to emphasise some aspect of the sitter's character. Greuze seems to have portrayed his sitter in this book as Apollo and he and most of the later neoclassic artists featured would also add value to their paintings by incorporating references derived from Italian masters and from classical art in their portraits.

Such secular portraits may be produced for many reasons: to enhance the prestige of the sitter, to preserve a likeness for friends

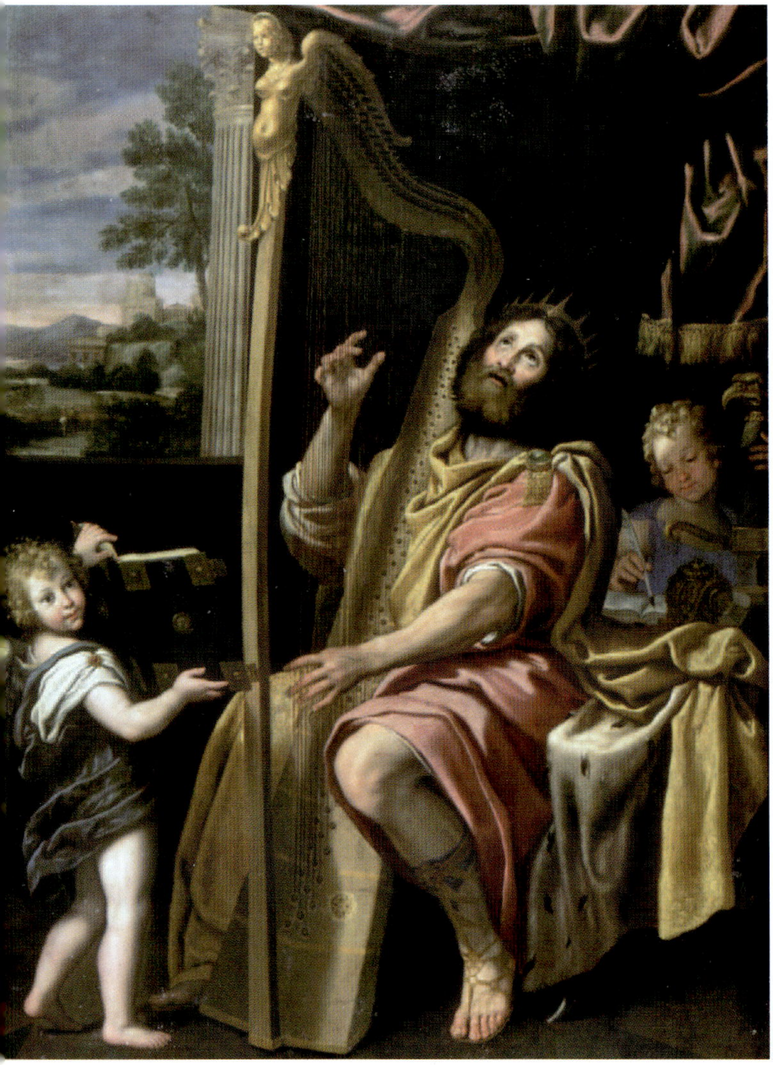

and family, to cement a sitter's relationship with his social circle, or, in the case of a lady, to indicate her feminine accomplishments and her suitability for marriage.

In the context under consideration in this book further agendas might include advertising the harp builder's art (as in Zampieri's famous image of David playing a triple harp – used today as a model for replicas of seventeenth-century instruments)[6] or emphasising the patron's wealth by ownership of a valuable instrument (as in Lanfranco's Venus).

Harps are quite common in portraiture as props for the sitter – possibly a situation initially inspired by the use of the lyre in Greek illustrations. Full-size harps were particularly useful from the late eighteenth century onwards, as tuning the instrument could provide a sound rationale for a lady to be pictured standing up, as well as serving as a foil for her figure. And aside from any design function, harps might be appropriate as metaphors for music, and by extension, love and sexual attraction.

Our first artist is one whose most famous portraits are full of complex allegory, the meaning of which, probably fairly obvious to the artist's contemporaries, can often be intriguingly obscure in the present day.

*King David with a harp*
Zampieri, early C17

---

1 The so-called *Utrecht Psalter*, compiled between 816 and 834 (actually from Hautvillers near Reims in Northern France) is accepted as the first medieval manuscript with drawings or paintings of harps.

2 Ernest Hébert and Edward Burne-Jones were both responsible for a number of images of harps in allegorical paintings (e.g. *La vierge au paradis* and *The Last Sleep of Arthur in Avalon* respectively).

3 Pierre Mignard's *Sainte Cécile chantant les louanges du seigneur* for example.

4 Roslyn Rensch is particularly comprehensive in her interpretations of such paintings.

5 But we don't know the identity of the sitters portrayed as harpists in Zampieri's *David*, Rembrant's *David and King Saul* or Ruben's picture of *King David playing the harp*. However, by contrast the last named painter's *Three Graces* of 1638 includes a portrait of his wife. [See also Lanfranco footnote below.]

6 Zampieri is said by Roslyn Blyn-Ladrew to have been a harp builder (as well as a front rank artist). See the Harp Blog http://www.celticharper.com/harpblog/.

# THE PORTRAITS

# Music and Mountaineering

## XYLOTECTUS (JOHANNES ZIMMERMANN), 1520

*attributed to Hans Holbein the Younger*

This famous picture of a harpist with a blank stare has long been attributed to Hans Holbein the younger. Son of a family of engravers and artists from Augsburg, Germany, Holbein moved to Basel in Switzerland, and then in later life to London where he became the painter for the Court of King Henry VIII. As such, he became one of the most celebrated portraitists of the age, and was responsible for many memorable images from that era including *The Ambassadors* and of course, imposing portraits of the king himself.

*A harpist says:*

"Judging from his expression, Xylotectus seems to have been rather a reluctant harpist."

Quite a lot is known about the sitter, sometimes called 'Xylotectus' (a latinisation of his German family name, which means 'carpenter'). Born into an aristocratic family, he grew up in the Swiss city of Lucerne, and was a member of a 'humanist' religious network which anticipated some of the ideas of Protestantism and focussed particularly on translating the Bible from the original Greek. Members of the network included Hans Holbein, Erasmus, Thomas More (whose family were Holbein's first sitters in London) and the preacher Myconius, with whom Xylotectus completed the first documented ascent of Mount Pilatus, near Lucerne in 1518.[1] It was not until 1523 that Xylotectus moved the 100 miles from Lucerne to Basel, where he was to work as a choirmaster, composer and teacher of classics. The young Hans Holbein had been in business as a portrait artist and engraver there for some years. As the painting is firmly dated 1520 by its inscription, Holbein might have painted this picture on an earlier visit by the harpist, or on a visit by the artist to Lucerne in that year.

It says quite a lot for the persistence of harp technique that the musician's hands are positioned much as one would place them today on an Irish harp: right hand playing the higher notes, left hand the lower.

The instrument itself can be described as a typical late medieval 'Gothic' type and it is similar to those in illustrations by van Meckenem, Dürer and Bosch (illustrated in the previous chapter). Although the harp shares the same general shape and number of strings as the slightly earlier instrument in Bosch's illustration, the strings are mounted differently on the frame and the soundboard is not of the same design. Unfortunately, it is not possible to see how the instrument is actually kept in position while being played. It may be resting against a thigh in the manner of the knee harp in Giovannino de' Grassi's illustration (shown in the previous chapter).

From the sitter's cloak with fine lining and felt hat, we see Xylotectus to be quite well to do, but probably not rich. The Latin inscription above the painting clearly identifies the sitter.[2]

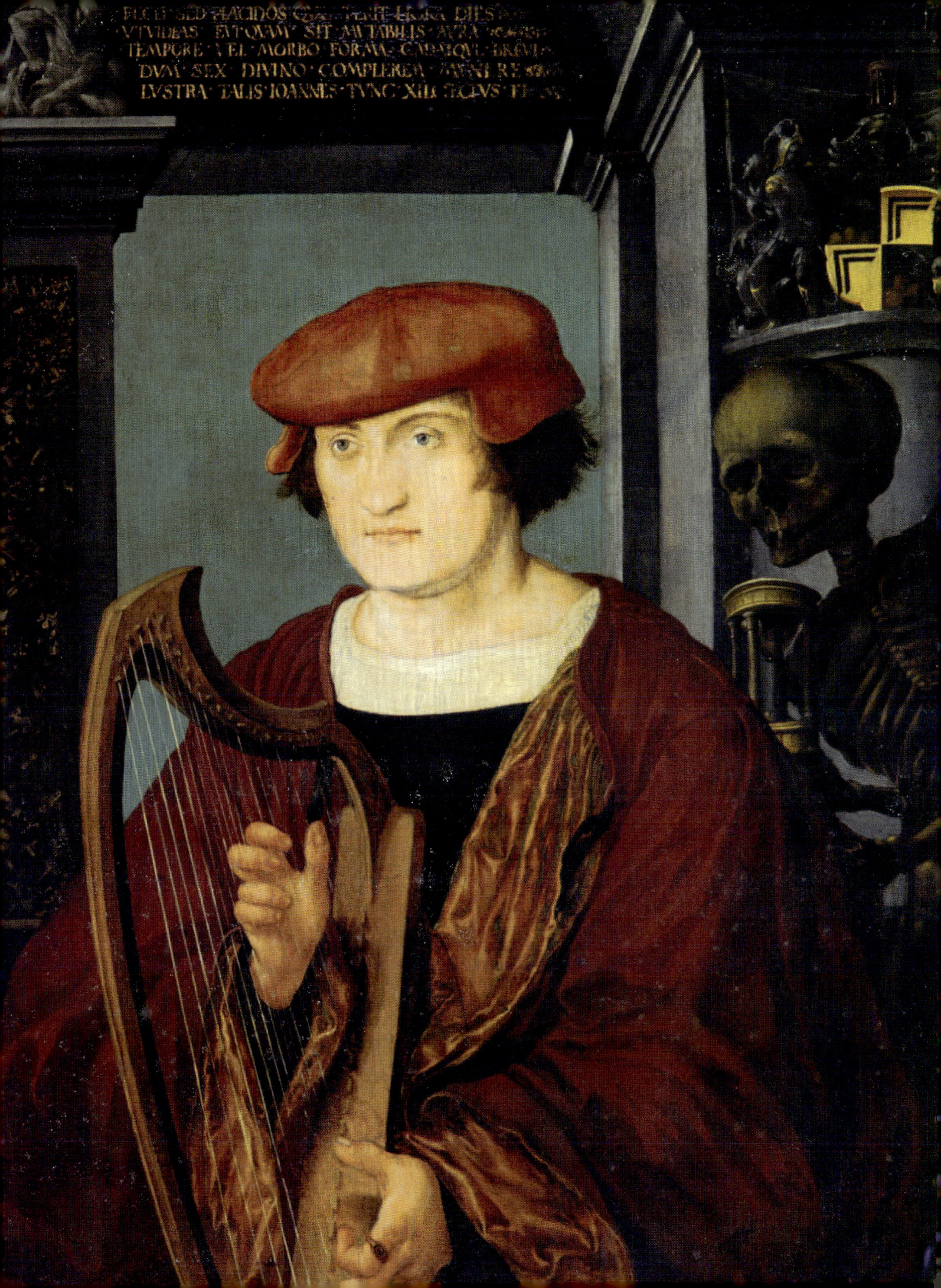
VTVIDEAS EVTQVAM SIT MVTABILIS AVRA
TEMPORE VEL MORBO FORMA
DVM SEX DIVINO COMPLEREM
LVSTRA TALIS IOANNES TVNC

Hans Holbein and contemporary artists often surrounded sitters with objects of symbolic interest. In the Xylotectus picture we see 'death' in the form of a complete skeleton gazing at the viewer with an hourglass from behind the harpist's left shoulder. The items in the portrait and the inscription lead us to the conclusion that the artist is telling us something about the transience of human existence. In Holbein's well-known picture *The Ambassadors* there is also a skull (in this case without the rest of the skeleton, and intriguingly distorted) together with some music, a flute-case, and a lute — complete with broken string. However, one has to admit that as far as facial expressions are concerned, even *The Ambassadors* is not a great deal more illuminating than *Xylotectus*.

But there is a problem.

If one compares the *quality* of Xylotectus's portrait with others by Hans Holbein, there is a wide disparity. Just take a look at the beauty and accuracy of Holbein's depiction of the lute in *The Ambassadors* and compare it with

*The Ambassadors*
Hans Holbein the younger, 1533

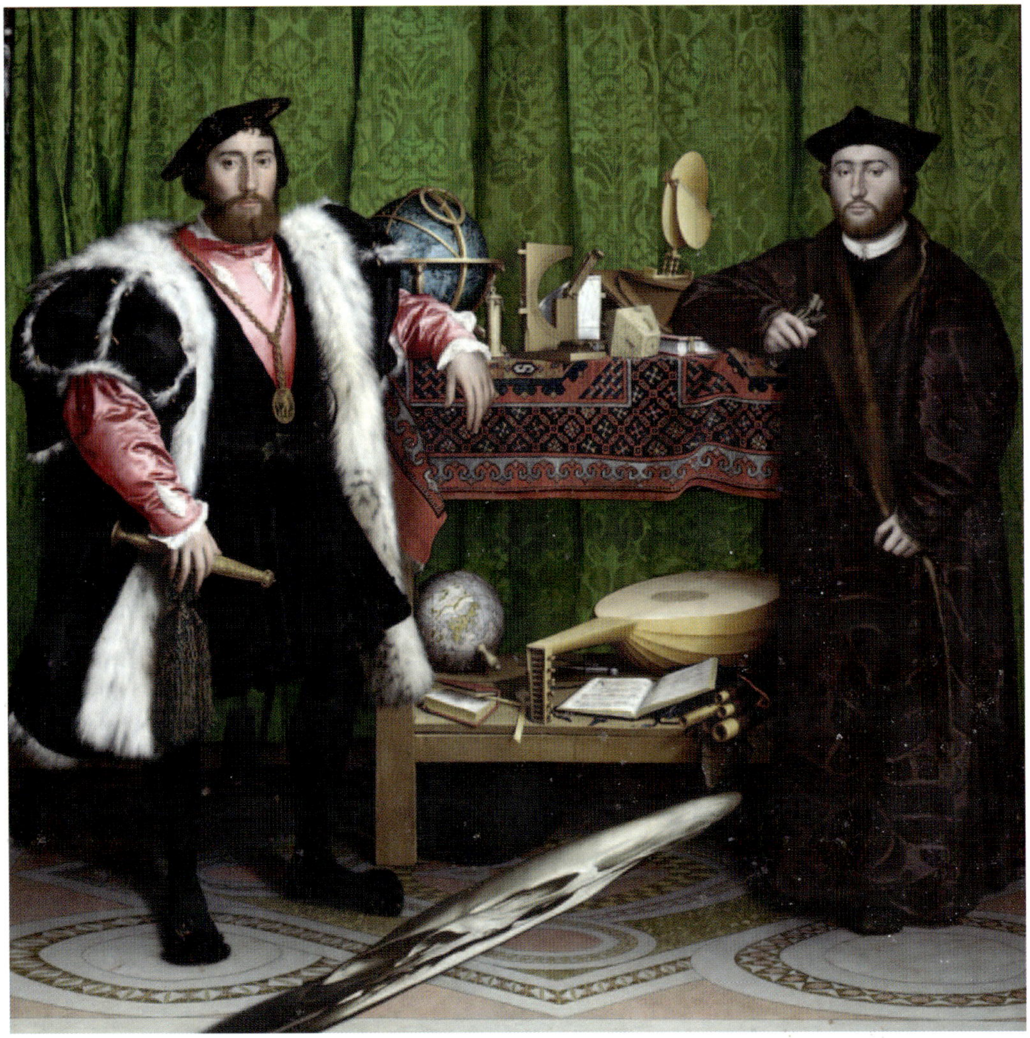

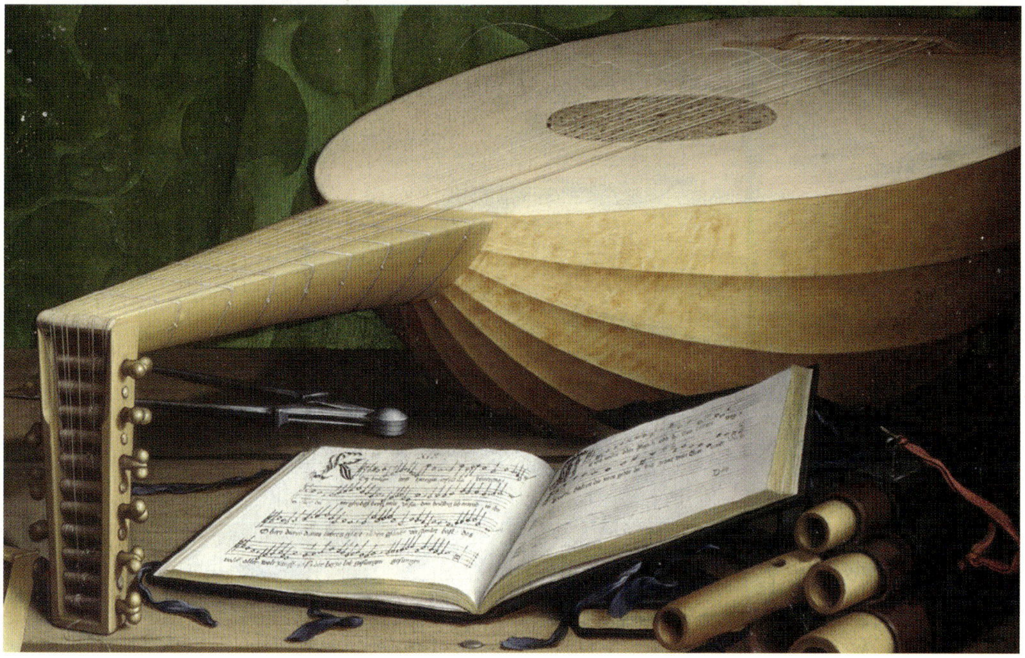

Detail from *The Ambassadors*
Hans Holbein the younger, 1533

the image of the harp in the Xylotectus portrait. The harp seems relatively clumsy and the perspective distorted. Of course, this might simply be that in the 13 intervening years Holbein had become more skilled, that he took more trouble over the later painting, or (as Hockney suggests), in the course of time he learnt how to use optical aids to assist his painting. But the disparity in quality is one of the reasons why the authorship of the painting is currently the subject of much conjecture.

The picture may be a collage, 'death', the image of the sitter and the instrument having been painted at different times, and *possibly* by different artists. Although Hans Holbein the younger may well have had a hand in it, aspects of the picture are similar to portraits by his brother Ambrosius, (who is believed to have died in 1519, so couldn't have been in on the completion), and an artist generally known by the monogram 'HF'. There was indeed an engraver called Hans Franck active in Basel around the 1520s who worked in a style similar to Holbein's and jointly with him decorated the book in which Xylotectus's mountaineering exploit was described. He seems to have painted images of 'death' pretty much identical to those in the portrait of Johannes Zimmermann.

Ongoing studies at the Germanisches Nationalmuseum in Nuremberg (where the painting is on permanent display), have involved examining infrared images of the painting itself and comparing details of the work of 'HF', Hans Holbein the younger and Ambrosius Holbein.

The jury is still out.

---

1 Vadianus records this in his edition of Pomponius Mela's treatise *De orbis situ libri tres…* published in Vienna in 1518. Partly in the nature of a geographical blog, this work also records a novel suggestion that the New World could be named after a certain Amerigo Vespucci.

2 'MDXX PINGERE FALLACEM NON PRAVA ?I?AYTIA FORMAM / FECIT SED PLACIDOS QVAE TERIT HORA DIES / VT VIDEAS ERI QVAM SIT MVTABILLIS AVRA / TEMPORE VEL MORBO FORMA CADATQVE BREVI / DVM SEX DIVINO COMPLEREM MVNERE LVSTRA / TALIS IOANNES TVNC XILOTECTUS ERAM'.

# The Naked Harpist

## ALLEGORIA DELLA MUSICA (Venus Playing The Harp), c1632

*Giovanni Lanfranco*

What's going on here? It's an amazing scene. The harp is balanced at a crazy angle and defies the laws of gravity. The harpist's posture is unrealistic beyond belief, and her dress code, unthinkable. The sitter seems to have been completely carried away by her own singing. This is pure fantasy, isn't it? No it isn't. The harp itself is entirely true to life. You can see this actual instrument in *Sala XIV* of the National Musical Instrument Museum in Rome, where it sits in all its gilded Baroque splendour, pretty much exactly as captured by Lanfranco.

*A harpist says:*

"The lovely fabrics in this picture soften a rather cumbersome looking instrument."

The picture is the exception in that it is not a portrait in the conventional sense of a likeness that tells us about a particular individual. It's a picture of a *harp*, with glamour added to make sure that no-one misses it. Marco Marazzoli (nicknamed *Marco dell'Arpa*) was a composer of importance, harpist and friend of Lanfranco. He was the owner of the magnificent triple harp[1] that is depicted, and he commissioned this painting. No surprises then as to why Venus, nominally the subject of the picture (and a god not particularly noted for her musical gifts) was portrayed playing this particular instrument.

In other Italian artistic centres, notably Venice, prostitutes were regularly hired to pose anonymously without their clothes in allegorical pictures. However, this seems not to have been the situation at that time in Rome (particularly not, when, as in the present case, the artist and patron were members of Cardinal Barberini's circle). And, of course, the portrayal of any *known* individual in such a state of undress would have been quite unthinkable.[2]

So this picture probably wasn't painted from life at all. In any case, a sitter would have had to invoke her godly powers to stop the harp toppling over. This may explain the rather artificial anonymous gaze and statuesque figure and colouring of the harpist, who, judging from the position of her exposed right foot and left toes, was blessed with improbably long legs.

In itself, nudity or semi-nudity was definitely acceptable so long as it was in an allegory of an event from classical mythology, or in an appropriate biblical context, such as Adam and Eve. This was particularly the case when the subject of the painting was nominally Venus (the goddess of love) who is seen here complete with attending cupids.

None of this, however, should distract the viewer from appreciating the effectiveness of the painting, which with its beautifully painted fabrics and bold swatches of red, blue, brown and pink is a dramatic example of Lanfranco's powerful skills.

The artist, born near Parma, worked in Rome and Naples as well as his hometown. He is regarded as one of the finest and most flamboyant Italian Baroque painters. His best-known work (aside from this painting) is the dramatic fresco on the cupola of *Sant'Andrea della Valle* in Rome — the

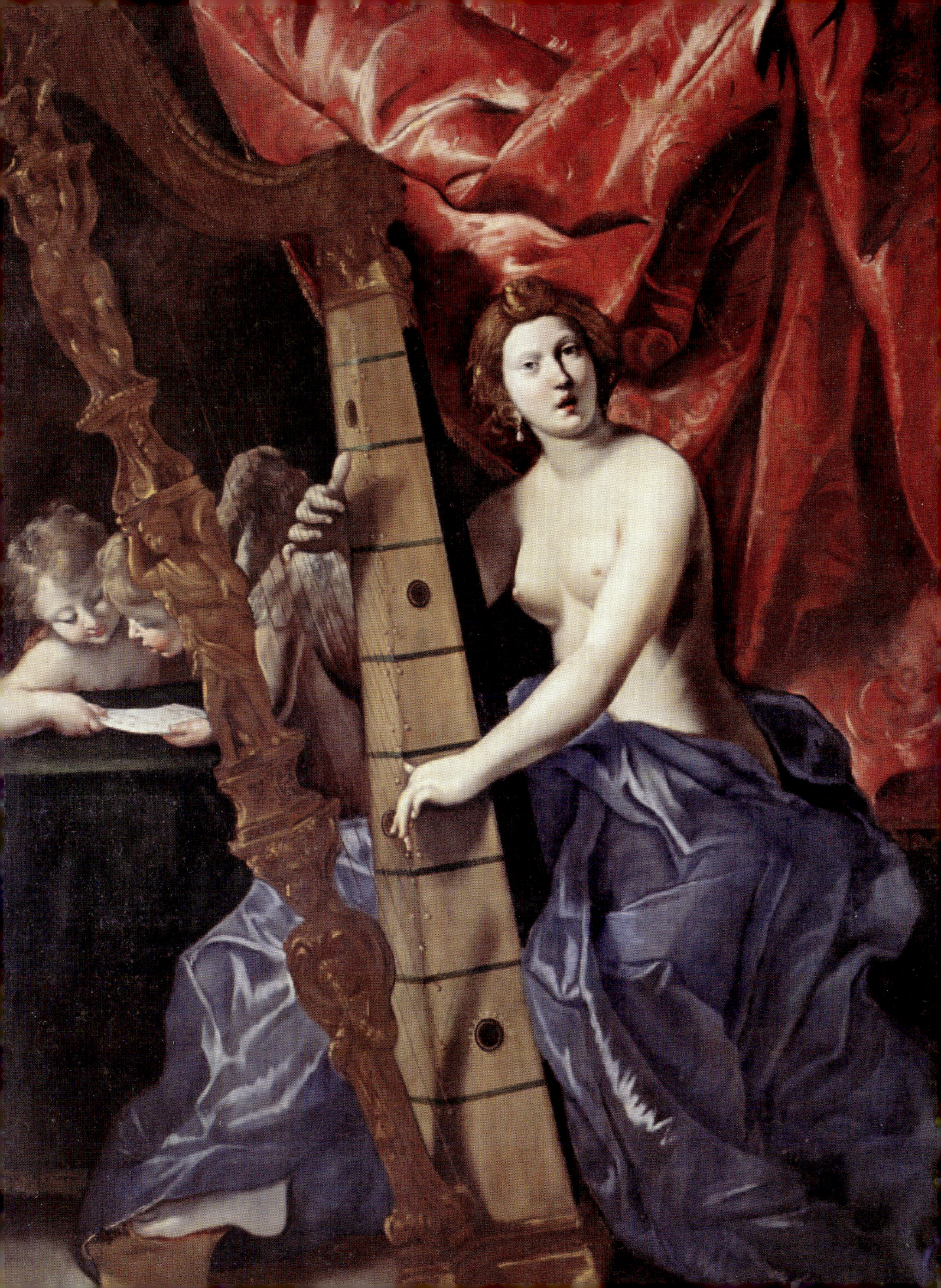

'theatrical' basilica where Puccini set the first act of the opera *Tosca*.

To return to the picture under consideration, some details of the musical allegory may not be obvious to the present day observer but it seems clear that, apart from any purpose the painting may have had to enhance Marazolli's prestige, Lanfranco is commenting on the power of harp-playing and singing to invoke love and passion.

Be that as it may, in the present case, portraying as it does Marazzoli's own magnificent harp, the owner would have found this splendid picture to be an excellent vehicle for his own self advertisement, demonstrating to all viewers that he owned the instrument which would probably have been without compare in Italy. With a picture such as this to exhibit, who would need a portrait?

This juxtaposition of the real with the unreal and of the erudite with the erotic is harmonious, and we might imagine that *Marco dell'Arpa* would have been well satisfied with the result of his commission.

---

1 A harp with three ranks (rows) of strings, the middle of which is tuned to play chromatic notes (that is the sharps and flats — the black notes on a piano keyboard). The most usual Italian term was 'arpa doppia' — 'doppia' being used here in the sense of 'large' (as in 'double bass'). Until the invention of the pedal harp in the early eighteenth century, harps with additional ranks of strings were the only ones that could easily play in different keys. Other illustrations of triple harps in this book are painted by Nuvolone, Hogarth, Ibbetson and (in the introduction) Zampieri.

2 Not a universal truth. For example, the wife of the Antwerp painter Peter Paul Rubens (1577-1640) is portrayed in his 'Three Graces' (1638) devoid of clothes. However, after his death, his young widow shipped the picture straight off to Madrid, where her likeness would almost certainly have been unrecognised.

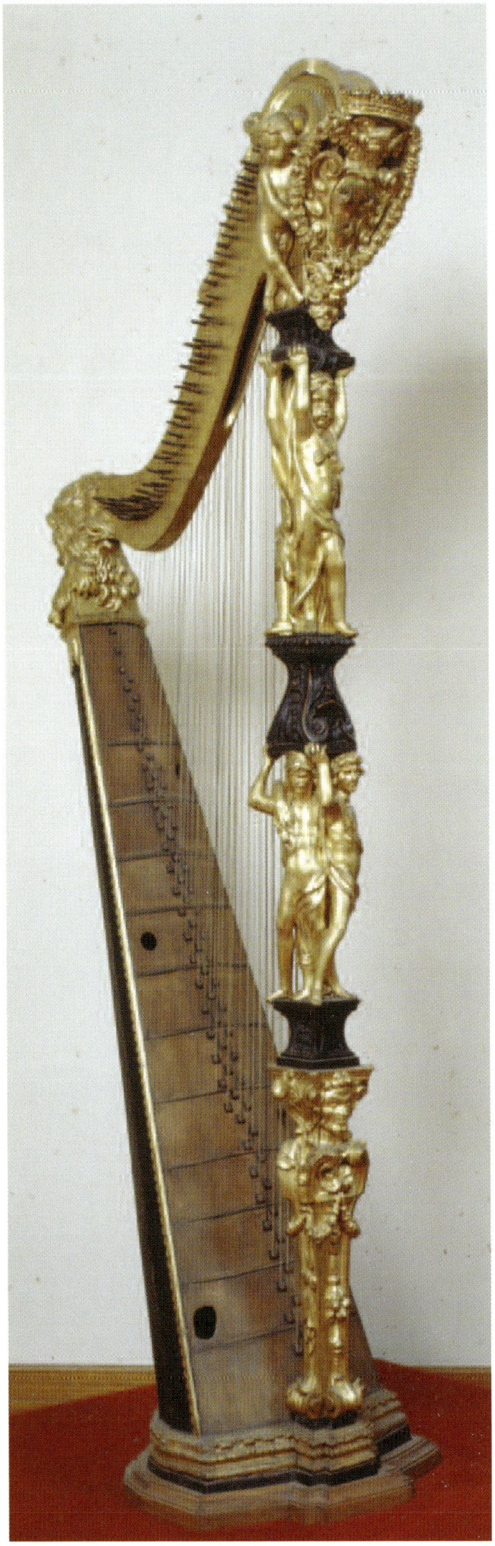

*The Barberini Harp*
(built between 1605 and 1620)
National Musical Instrument Museum, Rome

# A Family Affair

## THE ARTIST'S FAMILY, c1662

*Carlo Francesco Nuvolone*

This delightful family portrait will come as something of a surprise to anyone who has seen the examples of altarpieces by the Nuvolone family which abound in churches in and around Milan. In fact, doubt has been cast on the authorship of this painting, which seems closer to the more naturalistic tradition of portraiture prevailing in Flanders than to the northern Italian style. But in other paintings by this artist there is evidence of an acquaintance with Van Dyck's work,[1] and these famous inhabitants of the Brera gallery in Milan are now generally accepted as being the family of Carlo Francesco Nuvolone.

*A harpist says:*

"Was the harp really that tall – or was the harpist sitting on a very low stool?"

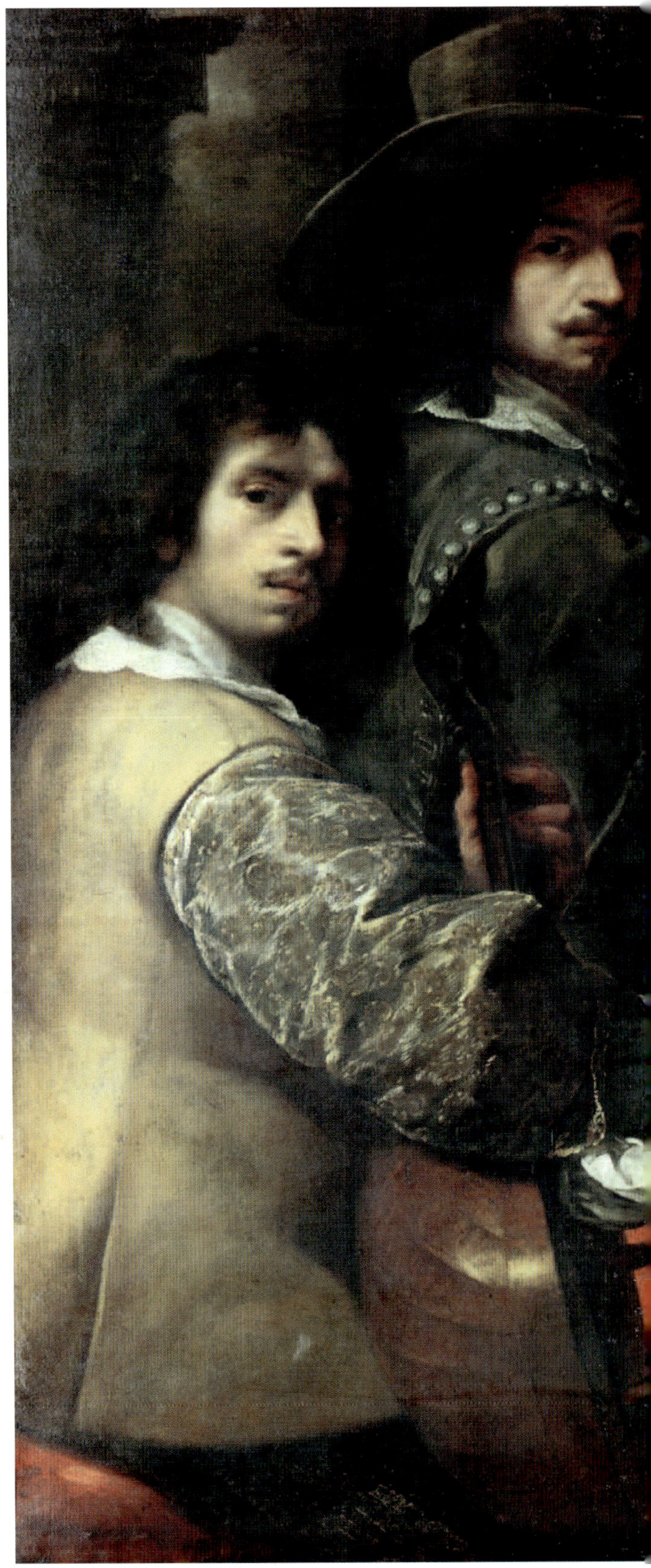

Carlo himself is seen at his easel emerging from the shadows, while his children appear to be in the middle of a jam session, with music that the party may have been practising placed on the table.

Taking centre stage is the artist's bejewelled and elegantly dressed daughter with eye-catchingly long black hair. The harp is

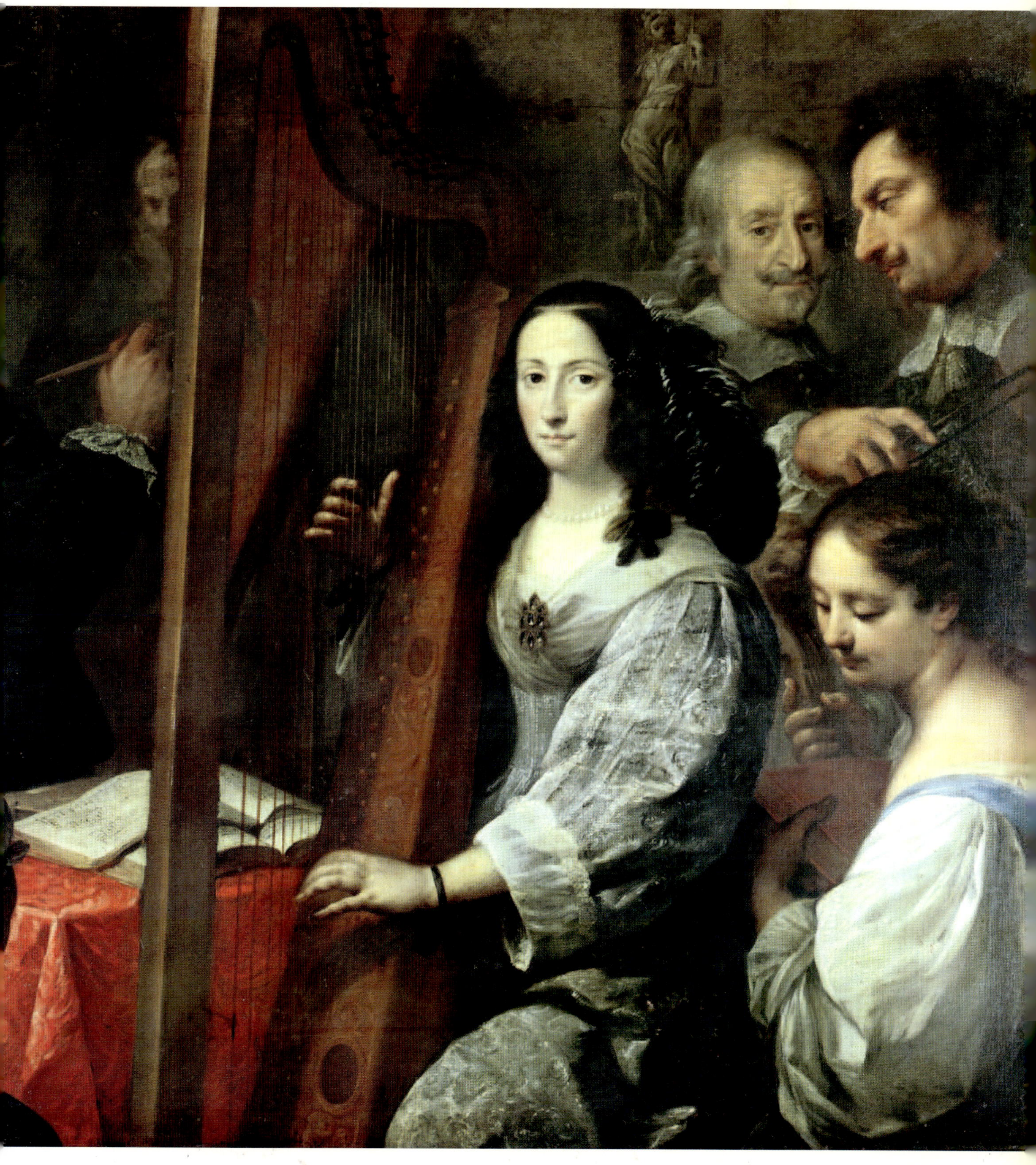

clearly drawn, if incomplete. Although comparable in height with the Barberini harp (illustrated in the previous chapter), its plain design can be regarded as rather more typical of the era — the harp having come into regular use in Italy as both a solo and continuo instrument. The gradually expanding sound box and clear pattern of string pegs and sound holes leave the identification of the instrument as a triple harp in no doubt.

Her brother is beautifully portrayed sitting alongside playing the lute. Perhaps it is her grandfather holding a 'cello bow and a sister clutching a triangular mandolin-type instrument.

The more you look at the picture in detail, the more it seems to be a collage of individual portraits, rather than one grouping. In particular, looking closely at the paintwork, the harpist seems to be very clearly demarcated from the sitters on her left, and there is also a stylistic distinction between the two girls. (Just look at the skin tones, for example.)

The informality of the sitters is delightful. The painter, lute-player and harpist look directly at the viewer, pausing from their activity as if for a photograph; whereas one of the two gentlemen in the background and the second daughter appear to be completely unaware of what is going on.

Although the costumes of all the well-to-do sitters are impressive, there is no empty display of finery. Ultimately the subtlety of the overall colour scheme — browns, greys, white, a touch of blue and red — bestows on the family a sense of quiet introspection.

---

1 Anthony van Dyck (1599-1641) an artist from Antwerp (in present day Belgium), who was a pupil of Rubens. He travelled in Italy, working as a portraitist before moving to London to paint at the Court of Charles I.

# What He Saw Was What You Got

## DAVID LEWIS , c1732

*William Hogarth*

Not many famous people have a roundabout named after them, and very few of them are artists. But driving from London towards Heathrow Airport, just as the busy streets give way to the M4 viaduct, the Hogarth Roundabout is encountered. This massive traffic junction lies just yards from the former Chiswick country house of one of England's greatest painters.

*A harpist says:*

"Of all the harpists in the book, this is the one I would most like to have heard play."

Hogarth is best known for his moralistic prints, the most famous of which formed the series *The Rake's Progress*. These theatrical depictions of everyday life were packed with humour, perceptive caricature, creative detail and a good deal of vulgarity. They made him famous in his own time, and gained him an international prestige which his name has continued to bear up to the present day. In the twentieth century the story was set to music by Stravinsky with libretto by WH Auden.

This is an appropriate point to caution the reader against the comfortable view that the harp was an instrument invariably associated with genteel social circles. This is because in the only other known picture of a harp by Hogarth, the instrument appears in the notorious brothel known as *The Rose Tavern* (the subject of the third picture in the *Rake's Progress* series). The blind harpist seems to be plucking away blissfully unaware of the frenzied orgy and general mayhem taking place elsewhere in the room. The instrument appears to be superficially similar to the one pictured opposite, but in this case additionally bears the figure of King David playing a harp on the fore-pillar.

But Hogarth's fame does not rest solely on his moralistic paintings and prints.

William Hogarth was the son of a poor innkeeper and was apprenticed to an engraver. He largely taught himself to work with paint, and had few artists on whom he could model his style, the exception being the most successful painter of the time, Sir James Thornhill. With the benefit of his own graphic and social skills, and ultimately the useful additional advantage of marriage to Thornhill's daughter, Hogarth managed to rise rapidly up the social hierarchy.

Until his time, portraiture had been an art form of low regard in England, where society favoured 'historical' pictures in the Italian style, mainly of scenes from classical mythology or the bible. Hogarth was disparaging about the use of such references in art, satirised them in his moral prints and avoided them in his portraits. In doing so, he found himself less favoured by some circles in the artistic community. But his legacy was the establishment of a distinctive 'English' style.

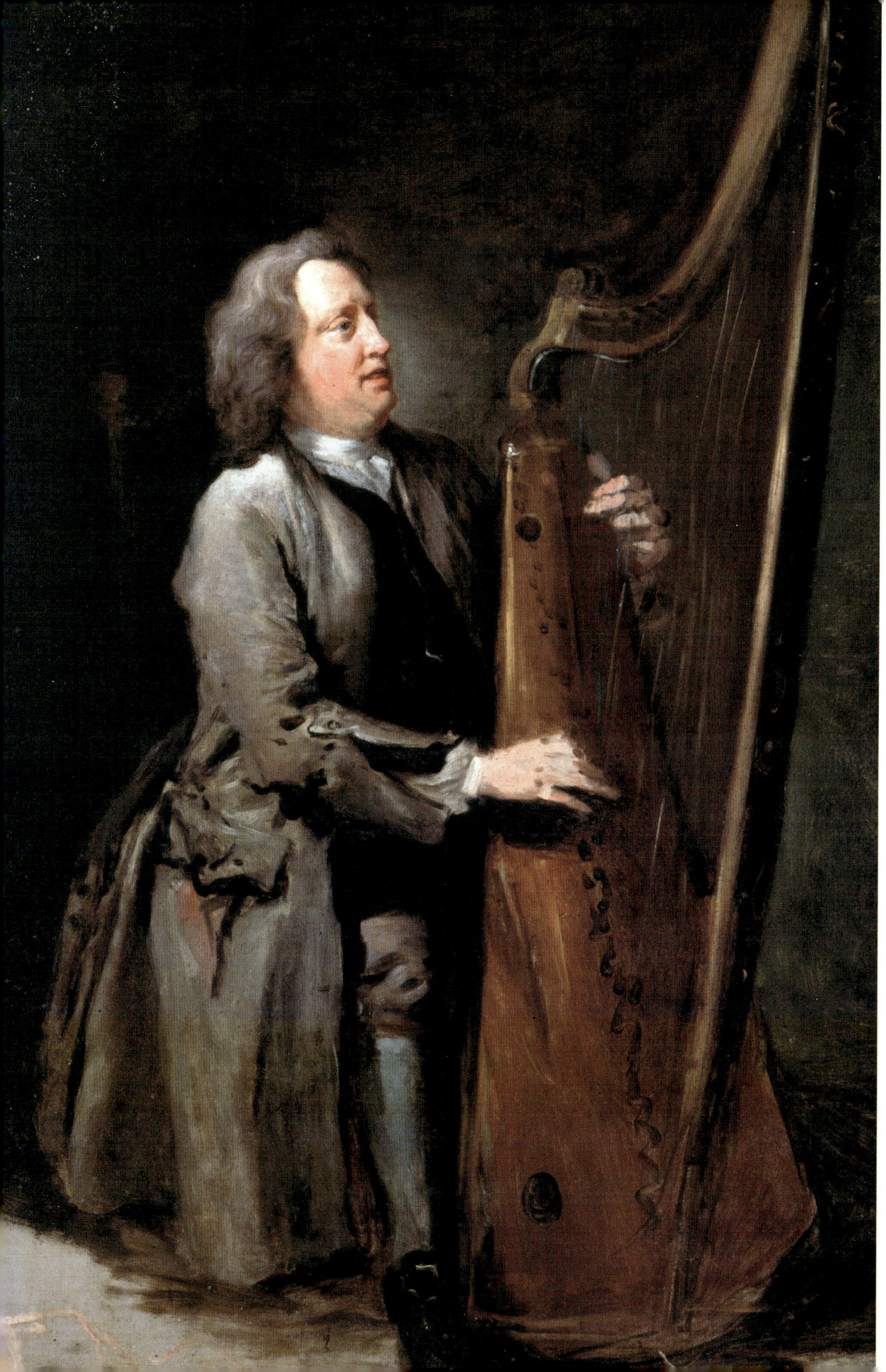

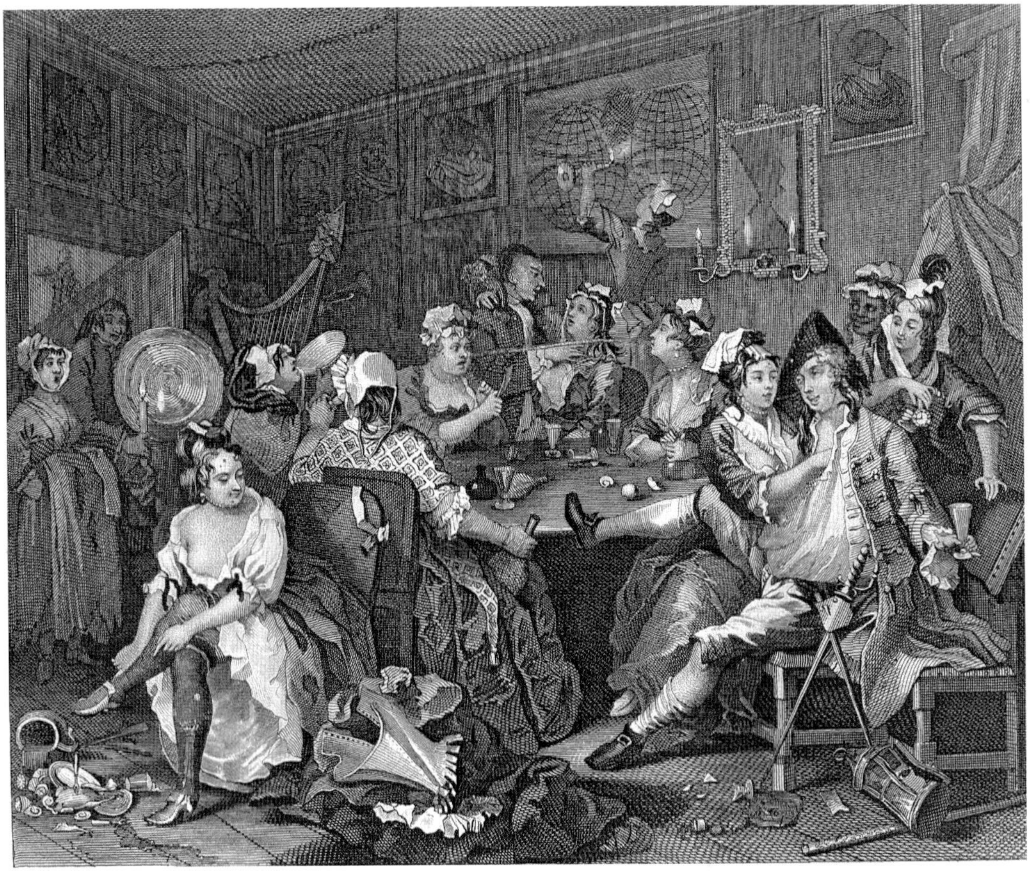

*The Rose Tavern*
WIlliam Hogarth, 1735

Hogarth was a lively and opinionated person, and in his portraits he did not feel bound to flatter his sitter — what he saw was definitely what you got. Perhaps for that reason he was financially relatively unsuccessful in that genre.

Those portraits that have come down to us manifest an approach that is very different from his 'moral' pictures, but they are equally highly admired. The quality of Hogarth's work established portraiture as an art form of value in its own right and the artist himself was by far the greatest English exponent of the genre in the early eighteenth century.

Hogarth's large and splendid portrait of a harpist 'in action' enlivens the walls of Aberdeen City Art Gallery. The picture displays the artist's interest in the dramatic use of light, focussing on the face of the harpist who is shown concentrating on his performance. It is a sketch, not a fully finished painting, but that in itself adds an attractive impressionistic quality and sense of movement to the work. Look at the naturalness of the harpist's posture and strength of his fingers set against the strings. The harpist's disability is neither exaggerated nor minimised. It's like it is. There is enough detail in the face to see that the harpist is singing — perhaps (as in the Ibbotson scene shown later in this book) *penillion*, a particular kind of Welsh musical form in which the singer weaves his melody against a traditional tune played by the harp.

One can also observe the pattern of holes indicating that this is a harp with three rows of strings, and the instrument rests on the left shoulder, as was traditional for Welsh harpists when playing the triple harp. (Hogarth's brothel harpist and the Welsh harpist shown by Ibbetson also play on the left shoulder, whereas the earlier triple harpists portrayed by Zampieri, Lanfranco and Nuvolone play on the right.) The triple harp facilitated the playing of music in different keys (the middle row of strings taking the place of the black notes on the piano). The harp in this portrait forms an interesting comparison with the 'Nuvolone harp' of about 70 years earlier. Although possibly not as tall as the Italian instrument, it can be seen that it has a sound box that widens much more dramatically.

By this time triple harps were particularly associated with Welsh harpists, although they had originated in Italy. The instrument is here being played by David Lewis, a blind harpist to George II and one of a group of harpists from Wales (a number of whom were blind), who worked in London in the middle of the 18th century.

Blindness has throughout history been associated with harp playing — there are even illustrations of harpists with this disability in the ancient Egyptian tomb of Rameses III. Many famous harpists and composers for the instrument have been blind, among them Turlough O'Carolan (1670–1738) from Ireland and John Parry (1710–1782) from Wales.

The harpist in this portrait is said to be the father of Mrs Hogarth's Welsh cousin. Robin Simon suggests that the painting, or a fully finished version of it, may have been intended for domestic display — not for sale or supply to the sitter, who, of course, could not have appreciated it.

Hogarth worked in artistic circles that overlapped those of leading writers such as Henry Fielding, theatre people (notably his friend, the actor Garrick) and musicians (including Handel, his older contemporary). Both Hogarth and Handel were much involved in work for the Foundling Hospital charity: the artist was a founding governor and exhibited his pictures there, while the composer gave benefit performances of his works in the chapel. The two also both enjoyed royal patronage.

Simon speculates that the harpist called for in the great composer's oratorio *Esther* (first performed in 1732, around the time that this picture was painted) may have been David Lewis.

# A Quizzical Gaze

## ANGE-LAURENT DE LALIVE DE JULLY, c1759

*Jean-Baptiste Greuze*

Although it is a name that is now not so familiar in English speaking circles, Jean-Baptiste Greuze was a painter of the first rank and the leading portraitist in Paris in the mid eighteenth century. His unusual skills as an artist, and exceptional ability to portray psychological quality in his sitters are universally admired in art circles,[1] although his tendency to sentimentality is not fully in accord with modern taste.

*A harpist says:*

"What exquisite fingers this harpist has."

His work has a huge range and Greuze can be compared with Hogarth in his influence on later generations of artists including both Ducreux and David, featured later in this book.

Ange-Laurent de Lalive de Jully, a figure in Parisian financial and artistic circles in the 1750s and 60s whose prominence matched the length of his name, faces the viewer with a quizzical gaze and a rather contrived informal pose.

The statue at the back is of a Sibyl, a Greek prophetess. She would have been included as a symbol of erudition, and it has been suggested that Ange-Laurent is posing as Apollo, a patron of the arts (often portrayed with a lyre in classical images such as the Roman fresco illustrated in the introduction). The writing table and the stool are beautifully painted and there also seems to be a portfolio of paintings — a further indication of the sitter's interest in the arts. The rather fancy dressing gown is expertly depicted, and it is very similar if not identical to the one worn by Claude Henri Watelet in Greuze's most celebrated portrait, displayed in the Louvre.

This painting is one of the very first to depict a pedal harp.[2] How ironic then that the pedals are not actually shown! (According to Rensch more of the same instrument can be seen in Diderot's *Encyclopédie*.) One of Ange-Laurent's many talents was as a harpist, and this picture, like the others of male harpists in this book, is effective in showing the strength of his fingers. However, some of the details of the instrument itself are not so impressive.

The harp, strings and pillar are vertical in this painting. A harp would rarely be played in an absolutely vertical position, but his may be a compositional device to emphasise the curves and folds of the sitter and his gown. The base of the instrument may also have been omitted for compositional reasons. However, the neck of the instrument is not well drawn and no rationale can be found to justify that.

Among other well-known paintings of Greuze is that of the young Mozart on his first visit to Paris in 1763-1764. As the leading Parisian artist (and a friend of Baron von Grimm who arranged Mozart's visit to the city), Greuze would have been the obvious choice to paint it. It is by far the finest portrait of Mozart as a child. Although not similar to other better-known portraits, it has recently been shown by Martin Braun almost certainly to be a genuine likeness.

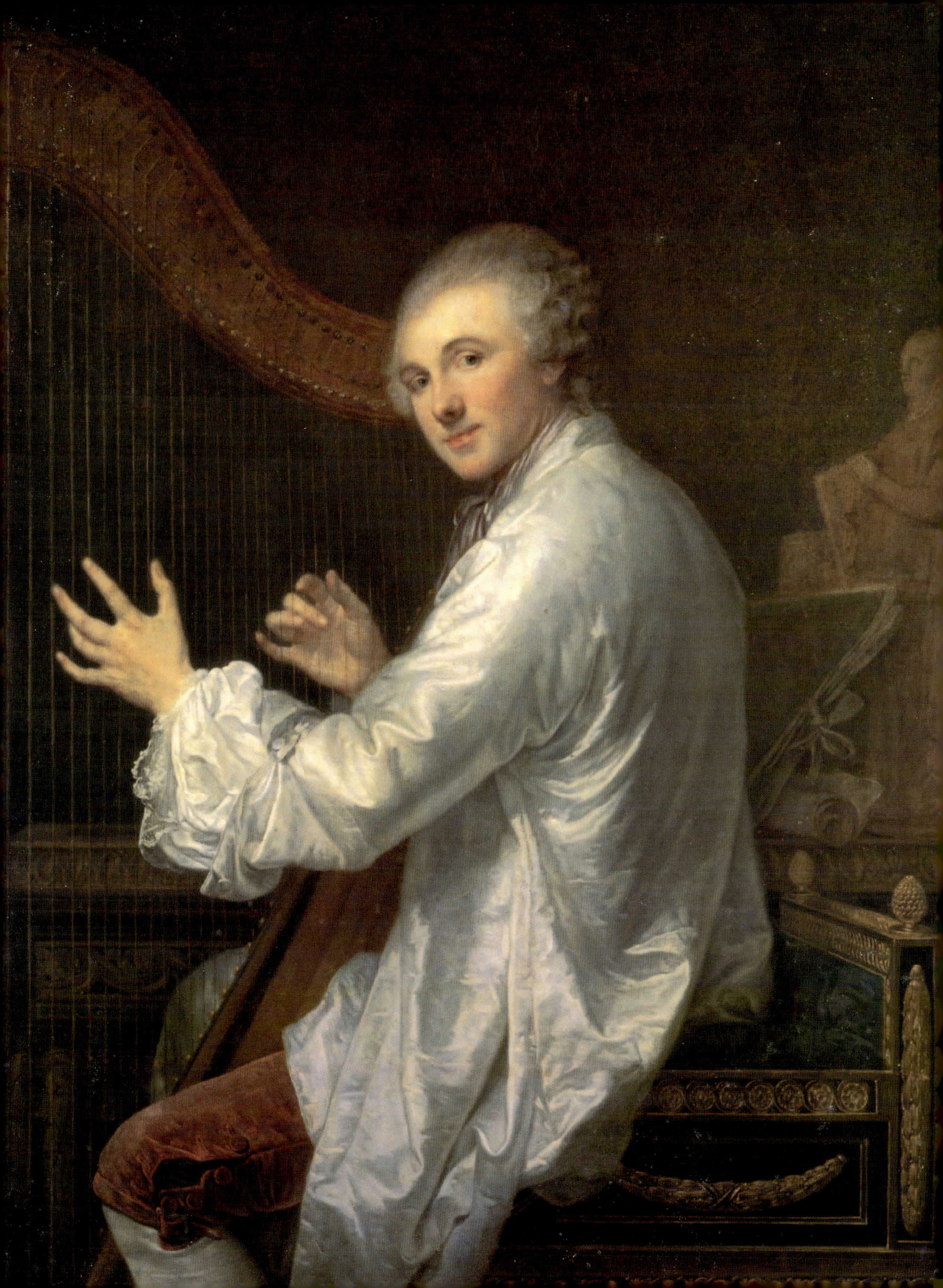

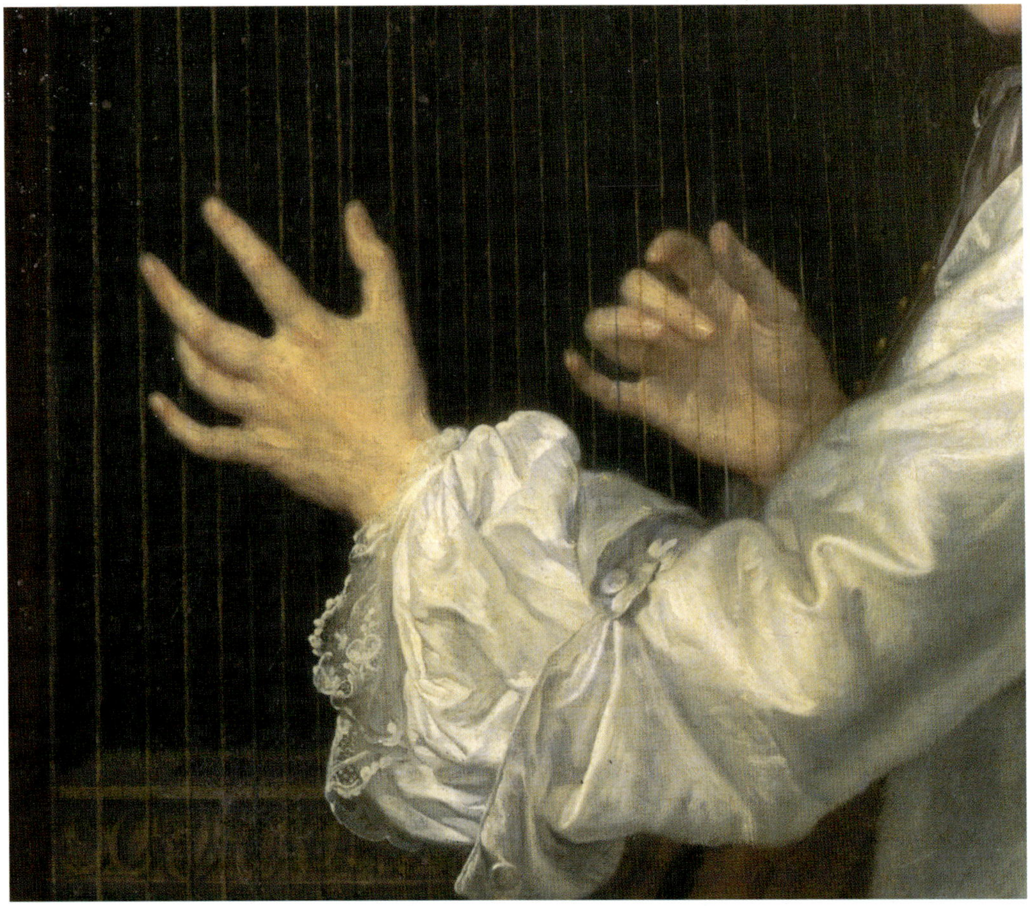

Detail from *Ange-Laurent de Lalive de Jully*

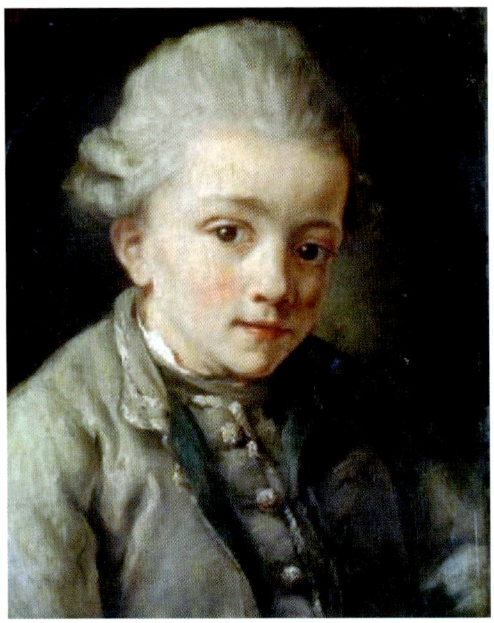

*Wolfgang Amadeus Mozart*
Jean-Baptiste Greuze, c1763

[1] Greuze's reputation also extended to the world of fiction. In chapter 2 of Conan Doyle's story *The Valley of Fear* Sherlock Holmes refers to Greuze when discussing Professor Moriarty's wealth and his ownership of one of the artist's paintings: 'Modern criticism has more than indorsed the high opinion formed of him by his contemporaries.'

[2] The invention of the pedal mechanism, which raised or lowered a set of individual notes by a semitone (that is, all the Fs or Bs for example) made it possible to play in different keys without the technical difficulties associated with negotiating the triple harp's three ranks of strings.

# A Pretty Young Woman

## THE COUNTESS OF EGLINTON, 1777

*Sir Joshua Reynolds*

'A young woman, pretty, lively, with a harp as elegant as herself, and both placed near a window, cut down to the ground, and opening on a little lawn, surrounded by shrubs in the rich foliage of summer, was enough to catch any man's heart.' [1] Jane Austen writes from a Regency perspective,[2] and this picture is a good deal earlier, but the sentiment is clear and has a resonance with most of the portraits of the ladies in this collection (most obviously that by Sully): when a harp is pictured in association with a young woman it contributes to her attractiveness and sexual appeal.

*A harpist says:*

"The harp complements the lovely dress, but it doesn't look like a playable instrument to me."

Here, the landscape in the background, the steps, the classical pillars and the curtain are part of Reynolds' successful attempt to add value to his portrait by introducing elements of Italian 'history' painting much admired by the British aristocracy. Indeed in this portrait he may be alluding to Saint Cecilia. It was Hogarth who put English portraiture on the map, but it was Reynolds who managed to convince the movers and shakers of English society that a portrait on the wall with these additions was an essential part of their home decorations.

Sir Joshua had studied in Italy and was rather sniffy about Hogarth's skills. As first president of the Royal Academy when it was founded in 1768 it was clear who had by that time become the Number One painter in Britain.

The portrait is imbued with the effortless elegance and sureness of touch characteristic of Sir Joshua's mature style. With her hair very definitely 'up' as was the fashion, the young and beautiful Eleonora, Countess of Eglinton, wife (and cousin) of the 12th Earl of Eglinton, is gazing dreamily to one side, music dumped unceremoniously on the floor. It must be said that she seems to be making only a halfhearted attempt to play the instrument (unless perhaps she is striking a harmonic with her left hand).

The 30-string harp, which has no pedal action, looks rather too fragile to be worthy of serious playing but does have an impressive bust at the top of the fore-pillar. Its lines and colour complement Lady Eleonora and her sumptuous dress and shawl. As was the fashion in earlier Italian and Netherlandish portraits, the pulled back curtain creates depth and a '*trompe-l'œil*' (literally 'trick of the eye') effect: this can assist in simulating reality by making the viewer think he or she is actually there, looking in on the real person.

The family home and seat was at Eglinton in Ayrshire, and the Countess was from nearby Bourtree Hill, yet there is not the slightest hint of Scottishness in this portrait.

---

1 Jane Austen: Mansfield Park chapter 7, 1814.

2 1811 to 1820 when the Prince Regent (later George IV) ruled Britain in place of his ailing father George III.

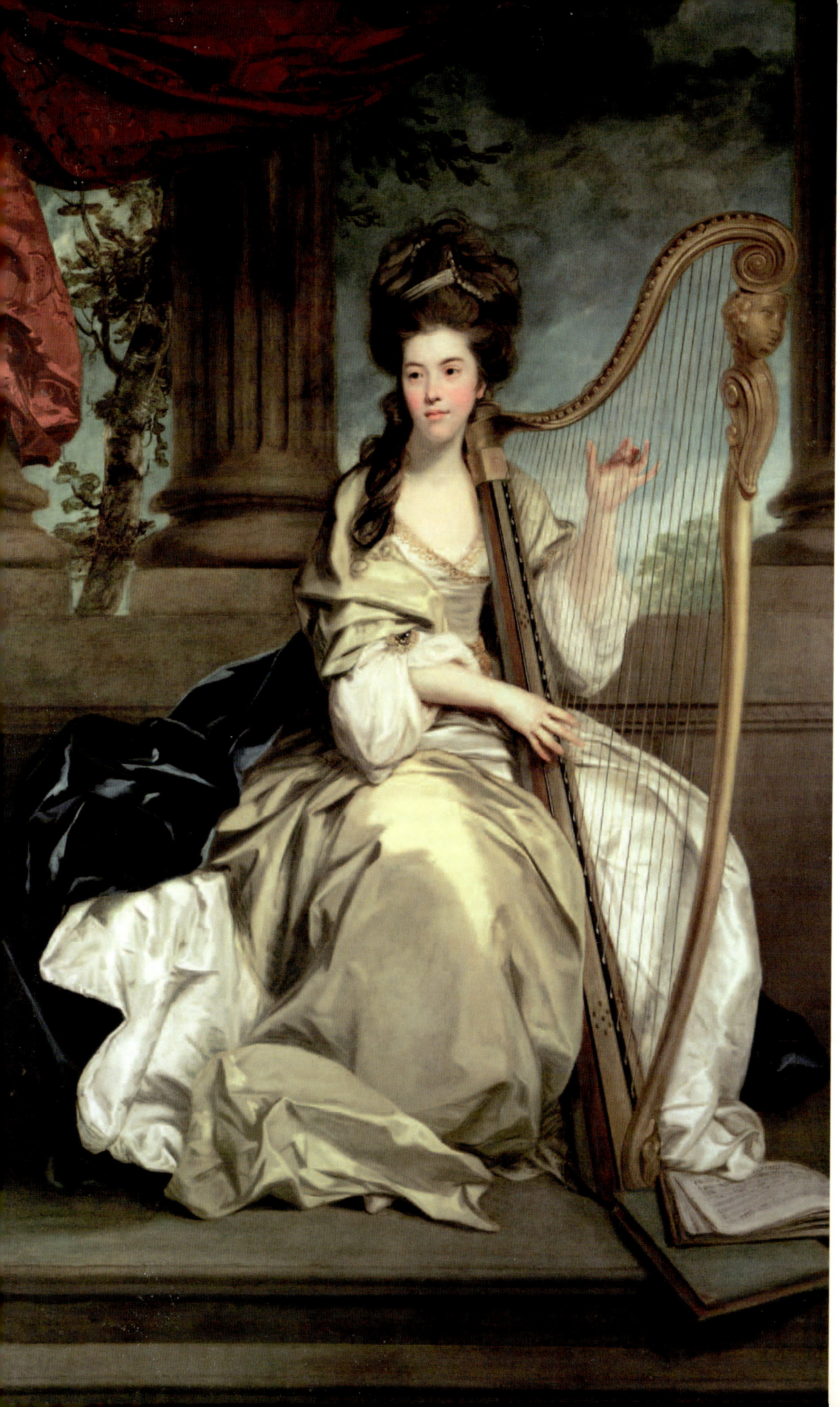

# Georgian Sensuality

## LOUISA, LADY CLARGES, 1778

*Thomas Gainsborough*

Thomas Gainsborough is the English portraitist of the Georgian period whose work is most enjoyed today. The son of a Suffolk schoolmaster, he impressed his father with his pencilling skills and at the age of 14 was sent off to London to study art. With encouragement from William Hogarth, Richard Wilson and others he was able to gain an income by drawing and painting from an early age, but it was only after he moved to Bath in 1759 that he managed to attract serious attention as a portraitist from leading members of Georgian society.

*A harpist says:*

"There's an air of tranquillity here – or is it boredom having to sit for such a long time?"

His delicate rococo colouring and loose brushwork imbue his paintings with a unique life and sensuality. When at work he stood back from his easel and painted with a long brush, and for that reason his work, like that of some impressionists, is often best observed from a distance. Gainsborough was himself a harpist and a friend of many in artistic and musical circles. A number of leading musicians of the day feature in his finest pictures. These include the best known image of the composer JC Bach (son of Johann Sebastian), shown below, and the magnificent double portrait of the distinguished singers Elizabeth and Mary Linley, which hangs in the entrance hall of Dulwich Picture Gallery.

Although his brilliance became universally recognised in the artistic world and he was a favourite of the Royal Family, Gainsborough was not always able to maintain good relations with the art establishment. Something of a free spirit and never an 'academic' painter, he fell out with Sir Joshua Reynolds and the Royal Academy in 1777 following a spat about the positioning of his pictures in the summer exhibition.

This portrait of Louisa, Lady Clarges (his only painting of a harpist) is an excellent example of Gainsborough's portraiture. Louisa was a fine musician and in this picture she is clearly shown to be serious about her playing, perhaps belying Fanny Burney's comment (quoted by Ann Sumner) that she was 'sportive, heedless, happy, and when she chose it, captivating'. The instrument itself is depicted in good detail and is most definitely a functioning single action pedal harp, possibly by the Paris builder, Naderman. As such it is an interesting comparison with the preceding portrait by Gainsborough's older contemporary, where the instrument's role hardly goes beyond that of an ornament. Louisa's face is beautifully painted; her hair is 'up' and decorated with pearls, her complexion luminous.

According to Ann Griffiths (also as quoted by Sumner) her stylised hands are shown to be employing the new five-finger playing technique, taught by Madame de Genlis, the celebrated French teacher and writer. (Madame de Genlis is illustrated in the triple portrait by Giroust in this book, where her pupil also seems to be employing this technique.) Unlike many of Gainsborough's

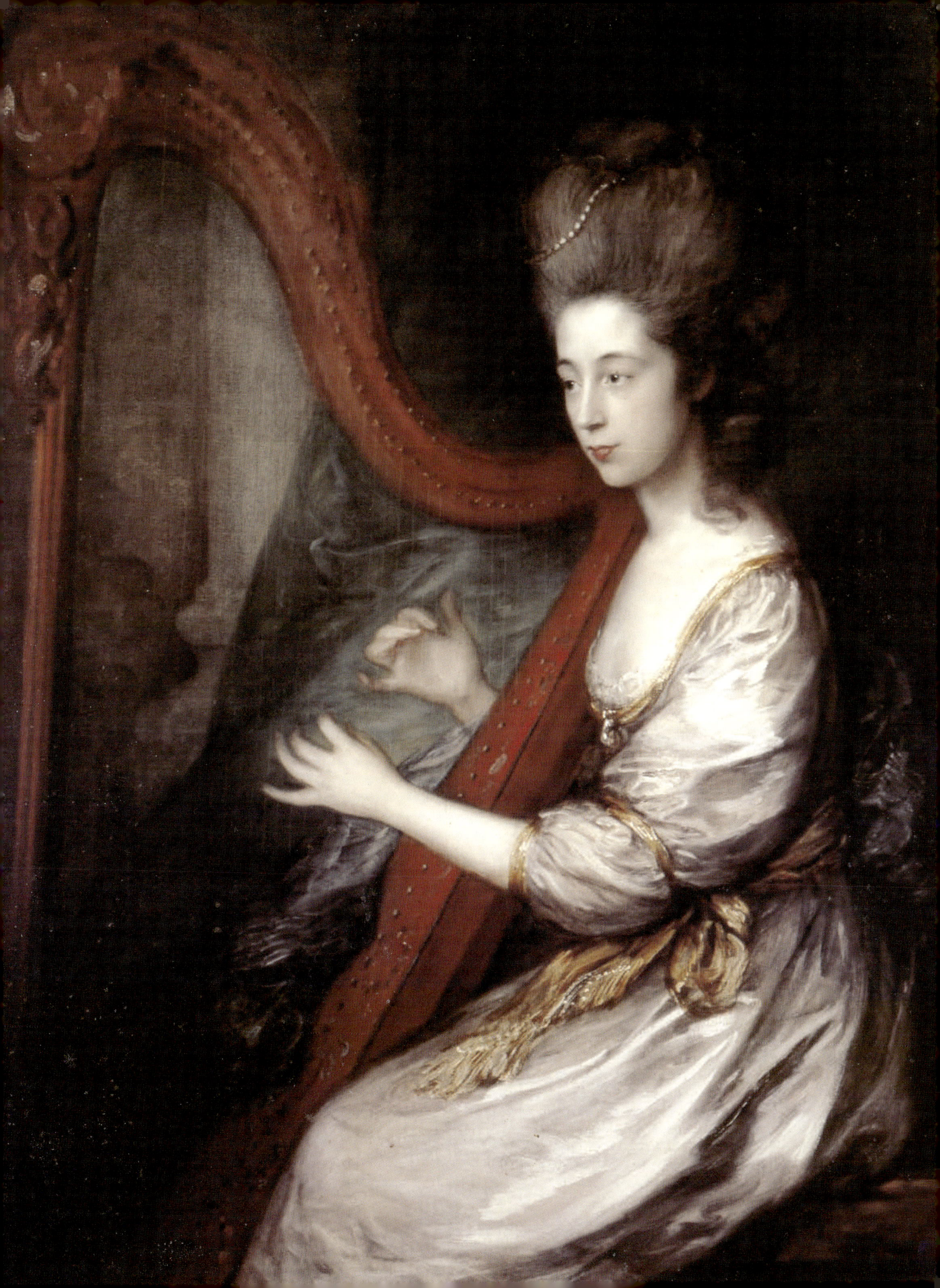

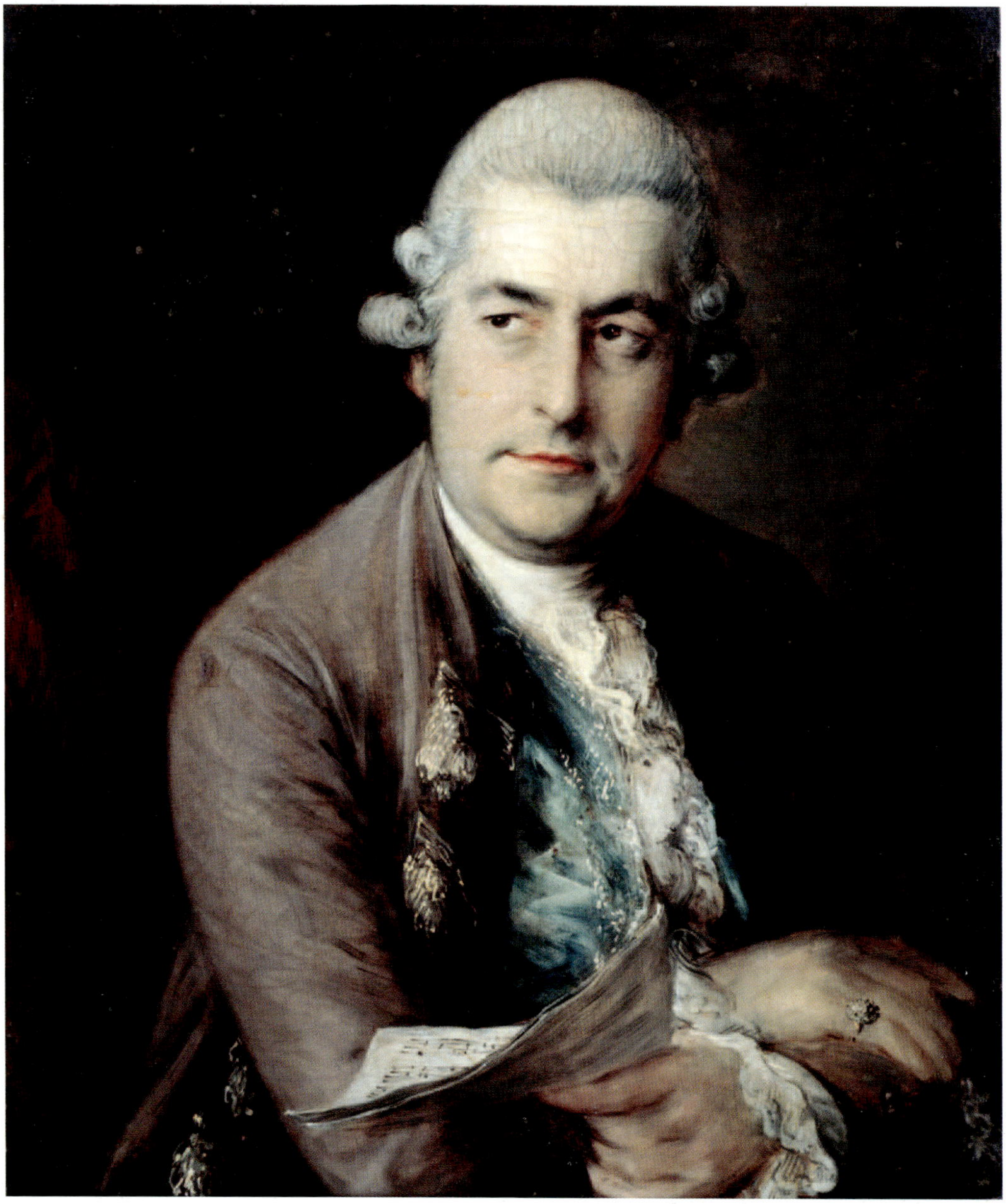

*Johann Christian Bach*
Thomas Gainsborough, 1776

most characteristic portraits, there is barely a hint of the countryside, and the inevitable classical pillar is rather murkily portrayed.

Louisa Clarges, (neé Skrine) became a proficient singer as well as a harpist, owned several instruments and made regular trips to Italy to pursue her musical interests. Of uncertain parentage, she married Sir Thomas Clarges in 1777 (after he had been turned down by Elizabeth Linley in favour of the dramatist Richard Sheridan) and this portrait may have been a wedding gift from her husband. Louisa Clarges and Sir Thomas promoted outstanding foreign musicians in

England and, unusually for the time, Lady Clarges continued her playing career after her marriage.

Following her husband's premature death in 1783 she spent a lot of time enjoying the vibrant cultural scene in Naples. While there she refused a proposal of marriage from Lord William Hamilton, the long-standing British Ambassador, who thereupon summoned the renowned beauty and actress Emma Lyon to be his mistress. (Emma was later to achieve notoriety in the same role for Lord Nelson – but only after marrying the said Lord Hamilton.) Louisa was one of the first purchasers of the new improved English-made Erard harps in 1792. She died in Richmond in 1809, probably while still in her early 40s.

# Revolution and Excitement

## THE HARP LESSON, c1790

*Antoine Giroust, copy by Jean Baptiste Mauzaisse (1843)*

What could be more tranquil? An aristocratic daughter playing the harp with her teacher, palatial surroundings, a beautiful assistant ready to turn the pages of the music?

*A harpist says:*

"I couldn't play my harp wearing such a broad-brimmed hat."

Nothing could be more misleading. The painting was first exhibited in 1791, just two years after the French Revolution had begun with the storming of the Bastille. Although Paris was temporarily settled enough for the annual *Salon* art exhibition to take place, King Louis XVI was under house arrest and all of France was about to be engulfed in turmoil. The 14-year-old girl playing the harp is Louise Marie Adélaïde Eugènie d'Orléans, the daughter of the Duke of Orléans. (The Orléans were the second most important family in France.) Although she wears the Phrygian hat, a symbol of the French Revolution, and the Duke was to vote for the execution of King, this was not enough to save him. Adélaïde's father was to face the guillotine at the beginning of the 'terror' just two years later.

In the 1780s the English miniaturist, Cosway, had drawn the same girl, this time in a genuinely peaceful family scene with her older brothers.

Richard Cosway was an artist who, in many ways, was to pave the trail for Sir Thomas Lawrence: born in the English West Country, he became the favoured painter of George, Prince of Wales (later to be the 'Prince Regent' and King George IV). He travelled widely and became a wildly popular miniaturist.

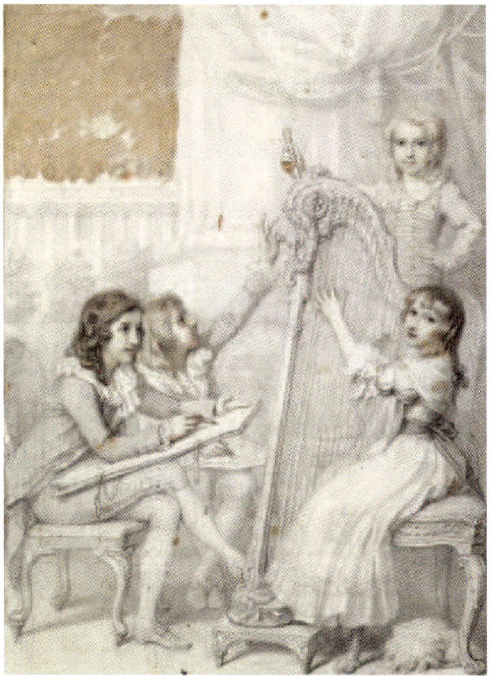

*Orléans Family Portrait*
Richard Cosway, c1786

This small sample of Cosway's prodigious talent is held in the *Musée Condé* in Chantilly, France. Although damaged (possibly by the need to erase a royalist image), and probably drawn as a sketch for a family portrait, the faces of all the children are complete and beautifully finished. Note that in this picture the harpist is not yet tall enough to play without the base placed underneath the instrument. Young Adélaïde, obviously the star of the show, is nevertheless mak-

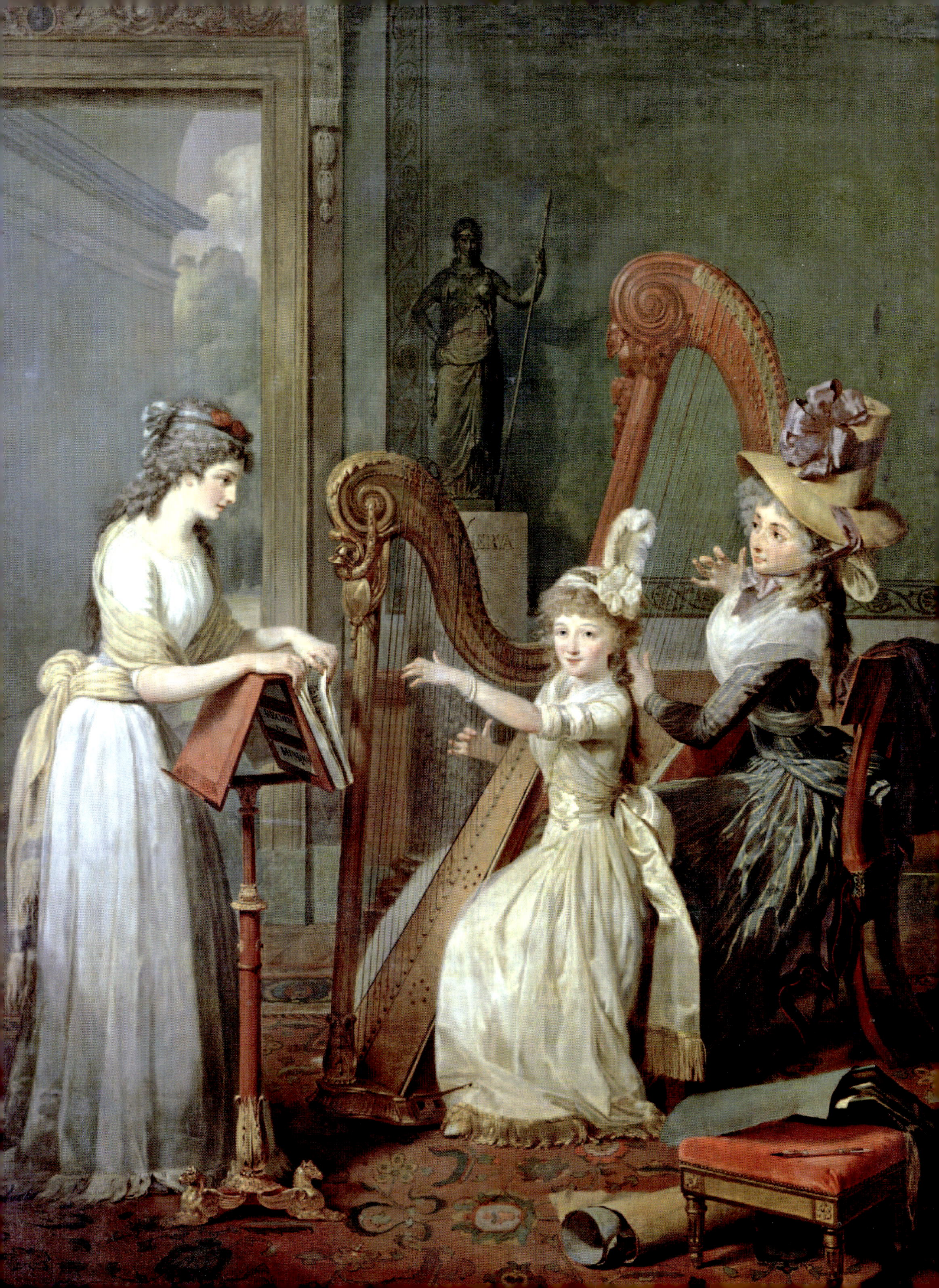
ERVA

ing a brave attempt to show off her prowess. As in the later Giroust image, she seems to be using a modern technique taught by Madame de Genlis employing all five fingers of her hand.

'Madame Adelaide', as she later became known, fled France first to England and then to Belgium, Switzerland and America. In one of a number of remarkable series of twists of fortune, she was shipwrecked in Guadeloupe in the French West Indies. While there she met and married a wealthy German businessman, George Casper von Schroeppel. The couple travelled to New York and lived in some style, first in New York City and then in Syracuse where their mansion is today listed as a National Historic Monument.

But her marriage was not happy and the revolution over, she separated from her husband and returned to France in 1814. In 1830, her older brother Louis-Phillipe (the boy who is standing up in Cosway's picture) was declared King of the French, and Madame Adelaide gained an official position in Paris as his adviser which she retained until her death in 1847 at the age of 70. During his reign a copy of the original triple portrait by Giroust was made by Jean-Baptiste Mauzaisse, and placed in the Royal collection. It now hangs in the *Musée national du château* in Versailles. It is reproductions of the Mauzaisse copy that have become so well known in the harp world.

The harp teacher with the broad-brimmed hat is the 45-year-old celebrated harpist Madame de Genlis, writer, educator, royal governess and follower of Rousseau, whose enlightened pedagogical methods included slide shows and field trips. As both a writer on educational matters and a prolific novelist, she became famous and successful in England while in exile there during the revolution. Jane Austen was among the many to be influenced by her ideas expressed both in her pedagogical works and her fiction. Madame de Genlis lived to the ripe old age of 84 — long enough to be able to return to France and see her former pupil Louis-Phillipe ascend the throne.

Turning the pages is the beautiful Pamela (*la belle Pamela*), Madame de Genlis' adopted (or possibly actual) daughter. Although her harp-playing prowess is not recorded, she was another fascinating historical figure. Pamela travelled to England with Madame de Genlis, was engaged to the playwright Sheridan, but married his compatriot, the Irish revolutionary Lord Edward Fitzgerald whom she had first met in Paris. Following her husband's death in prison in 1798 she fled Britain. She was later married to the American Consul in Hamburg, but (like the other two subjects of this tableau) died in Paris, in her case at the relatively young age of 58. Pamela is the subject of a historical novel *The Harp Lesson* by Emma Tennant, Pamela's great-great-great granddaughter.

Antoine Giroust was known as a fine painter of tableaux and portraits. This picture in the neoclassic 'academic' style shows two of the sizes of harp then in use in France, both of which are scroll crowned. They are most likely Naderman harps. Of the many family harp-making businesses operating in Paris at that time, Naderman was the one most closely associated with the French royal household and these harps are similar in design (although without painted decoration) to surviving examples. Classical details in the background include a statue of Minerva, goddess of wisdom and crafts.

By this time harps were very often to be found in the drawing rooms and *salons* of the wealthy in Britain and France, and harp playing was one of the more important skills that aristocratic ladies needed to acquire. The wives of both Louis XVI (Queen Marie Antoinette) and Napoleon (Empress Josephine) were harpists and beautiful instruments owned by these ladies are still in existence.

Josephine chose Joseph François Naderman, the son of the harp builder, as her teacher, and he became the first professor of harp at the Paris Conservatoire where her harp was long on display.

Among the other interesting historical details in the painting are the art materials, indicating that an art lesson is shortly to take place — perhaps also to be conducted by the redoubtable Madame de Genlis.

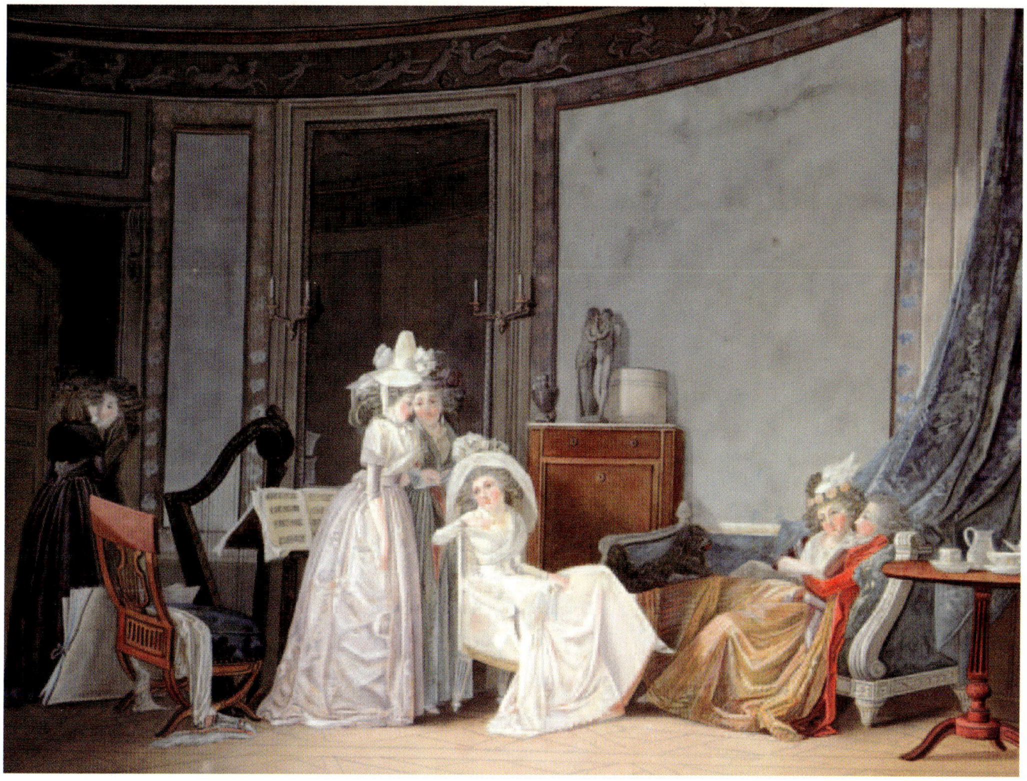

*Meeting in a Salon*
Jean Baptiste Mallet, 1790

# Tuning, Interrupted

## SELF-PORTRAIT, c1790

*Rose-Adélaïde Ducreux*

This sizzler of a picture is a self-portrait of significant historical interest. The artist, Rose-Adélaïde Ducreux, is one of a several female painters who exhibited in the Paris *Salon* of 1791 — the first year that members of the public were allowed to display their own paintings. These annual Parisian exhibitions, (like their London counterpart the Royal Academy summer exhibition) were lively and controversial affairs with massive attendances.

*A harpist says:*

"What perfect symmetry between harp and harpist!"

Rose-Adélaïde Ducreux grew up in a home that seems to have functioned rather as a *salon* and was frequented by other artists and musicians. Here the word is used in the sense of a grand house where artists and musicians would meet to exchange ideas, take part in *conversazzioni*, exhibit their work and give musical recitals. The artist Jean Baptiste Mallet portrayed a Paris salon of a rather more doubtful kind in 1790 in a picture now in the *Musée Marmottan* in Paris (see previous page).

Rose-Adélaïde's father Joseph painted both Louis XVI and Marie Antoinette and had an official position with the Royal Family. Along with his fellow painter at Court, Élisabeth Vigée-LeBrun, he found it prudent to leave France at the outbreak of the Revolution, but later returned and befriended the artist David, (an active supporter of the new *régime*). David's portrait of Rose-Adélaïde (as a young woman painting) hangs in the *Musée Des Beaux-Arts*, in Rouen. Joseph Ducreux included the successful romantic composer Méhul in his list of sitters as well as (remarkably given his previous artistic history) the revolutionary leader Robespierre.

Rose-Adélaïde was a musician and artist herself. She had stayed behind in Paris at the outbreak of the revolution in 1789. Few of her paintings are known, and this portrait was apparently misattributed (among others to Antoine Vestier and Vigée-LeBrun). But the Metropolitan Gallery of Art in New York, where the picture hangs, is now satisfied of the authenticity of the self-portrait.

Although it is Rose-Adélaïde's spectacular silk dress, hairstyle and remarkable corseted figure which first engages the observer's attention, the musical instrument itself is also meticulously painted.

Depicted with a harpist's eye, we can see that colours of the strings are distinguished (red for C and dark for F in the same way that they are today) and the pedals operating the single action are painted with almost photographic precision. In a fascinatingly realistic detail which it shares with the paintings by Greuze and David, the strings are shown sticking up above the tuning pins at the top of the instrument in a slightly untidy manner. The harp's scroll and fluted column (with decorated base) are similar to instruments still in existence which were made by Cousineau — a Parisian family firm of harp makers that were one of the many rivals to Naderman and who had aristocratic

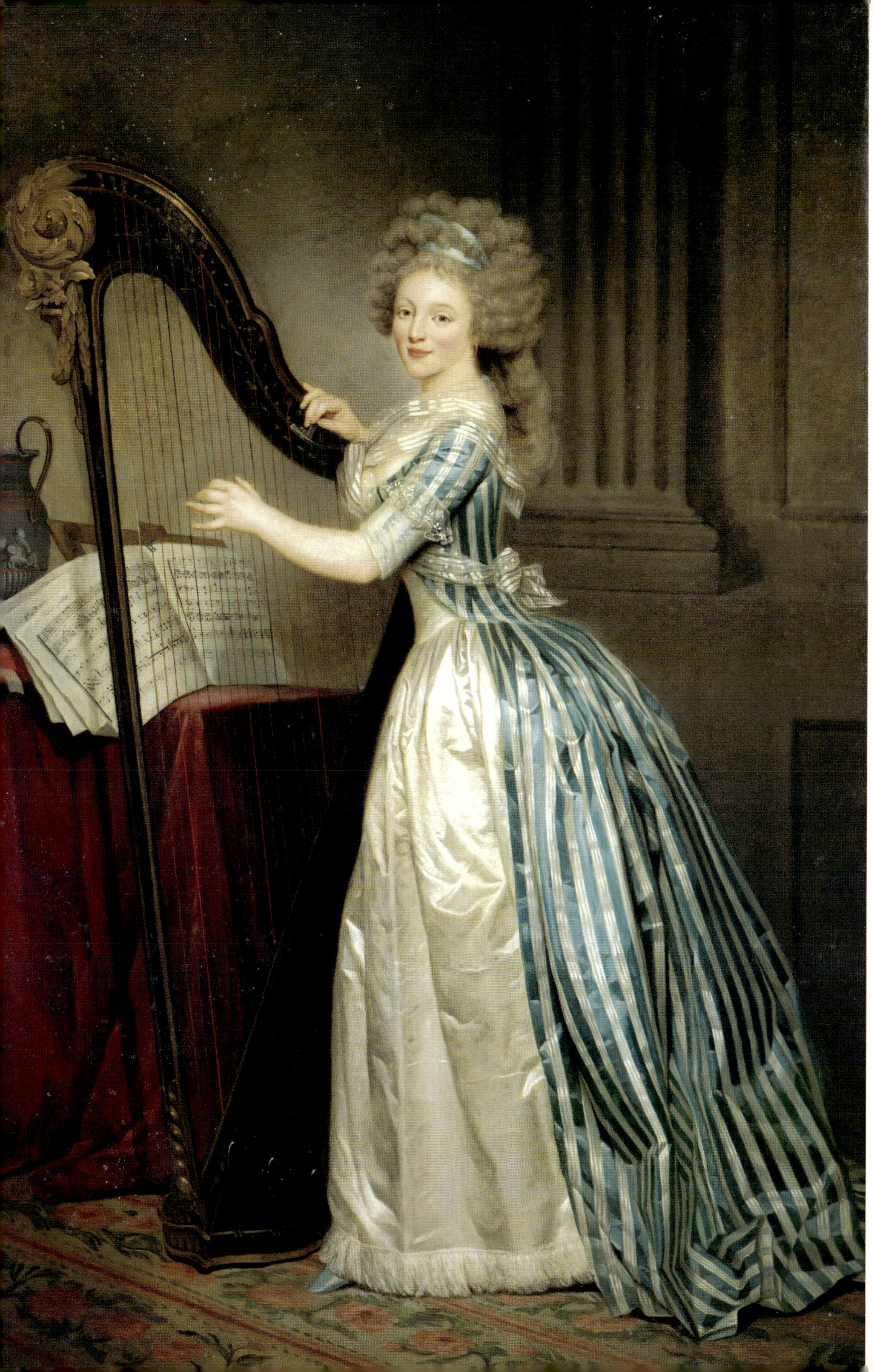

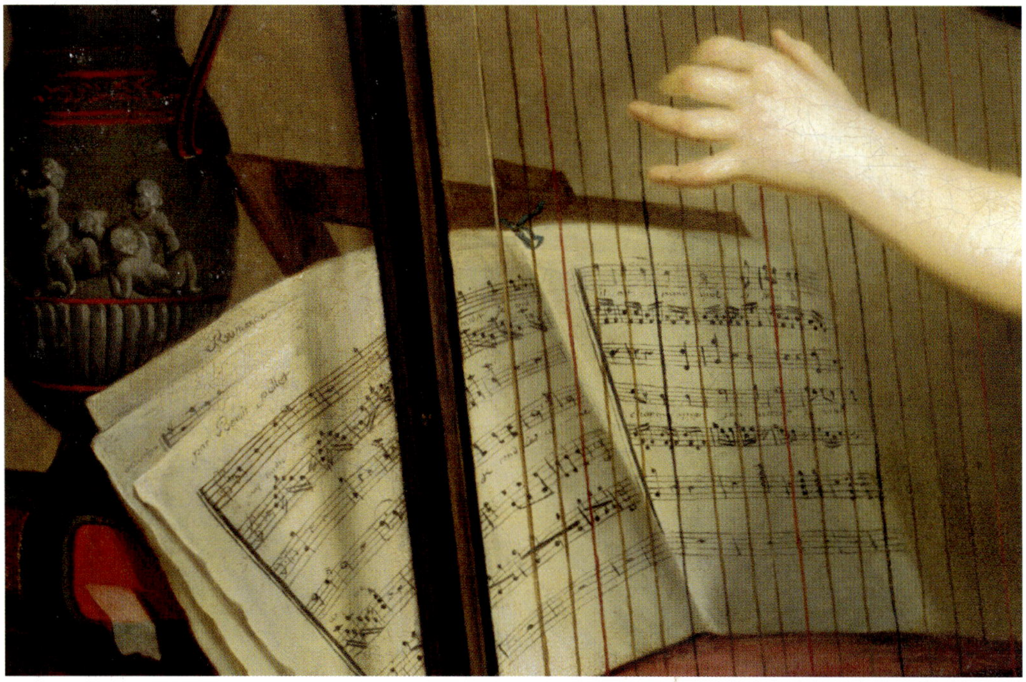

Detail from *Self Portrait, Rose-Adélaïde Ducreux*

connections that were nearly as good. The instrument is not being played, but it is not a mere prop for the subject: Rose-Adélaïde stands quite naturally, smiling as if pleased to be distracted by a visitor from checking the tuning. The tuning key is held in her right hand.

As a musician as well as a graphic artist this beautifully balanced neoclassical portrait would have been no mean advertisement for her varied talents. On the table rests a classical urn, a place-marked book on opera and a meticulously painted song about 'tender love'. Are we to gather from this that Mlle. Ducroix also sings to her own harp accompaniment?

The earlier attribution of the self-portrait to Antoine Vestier (1740–1824) is not surprising, as female artists were only just emerging from obscurity in late eighteenth century France. Around 1805 Vestier himself had painted a charming picture of a girl tuning the harp and a clear similarity of style can be observed, especially in the depiction of the sitter's face. Vestier's lovely portrait is to be seen in the municipal museum in Sens in northern Burgundy.

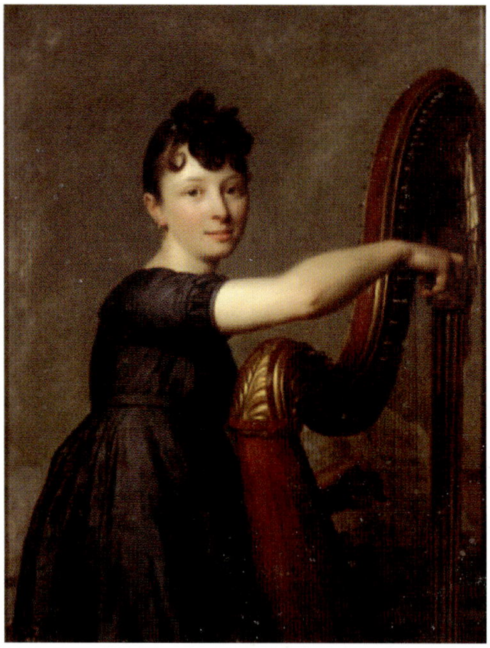

*A Young Harpist*
Antoine Vestier, 1805

# Peasants and Penillion

## PEASANTS SINGING WITH BLIND HARPIST JOHN SMITH, c1792

*Julius Caesar Ibbetson*

This delightful scene of music-making in the Welsh hills is an excellent example of work by the much-travelled Julius Caesar Ibbetson, a technically very adept painter, engraver, theatre designer — and forger.

**A harpist says:**

"This is hardly an ideal venue for a harp!"

A Yorkshireman by birth, he first came to attention with his copies of work by landscape artists such as Nicolaes Berchem and Richard Wilson. Later Ibbetson was able to adopt a more respectable (if less lucrative) career illustrating his own travels with scenes of rural life that he encountered. He visited both South Africa and Java, but he was also famous for scenes he painted on his visits closer to home, including Wales (in 1792) and the English Lake District.

This rather idealised scene shows a rocky outcrop near Conwy in North Wales. Perhaps it's on the edge of an *eisteddfod* or a fair. Some of the peasants are singing *penillion* accompanied by the blind harpist John Smith, while others are pictured listening to the impromptu concert. A second harpist and a pair of dancers can be seen in the background. The watercolour repays careful study, as it is full of lively characterisation and keen social observation.

The harp is not shown in great detail, but it is being played on the left shoulder, typical of the way that the triple harp was played in Wales.

The undoubted skill of the artist is at its best in the nostalgic scene of nearby Conwy Castle probably sketched on the same tour. The chiaroscuro (light and dark) technique he learnt from forging Dutch artists is put to good use in the depiction of the moonlit cloudscape shining over the romanticised castle. He may have pictured himself painting in the foreground, making a sketch of the ferry.

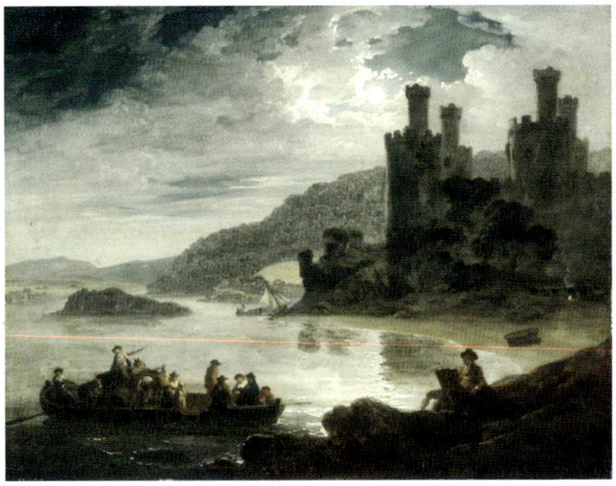

*Conwy Castle*
Julius Caesar Ibbetson, 1794

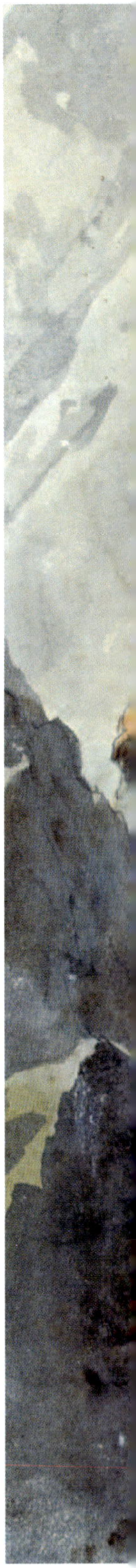

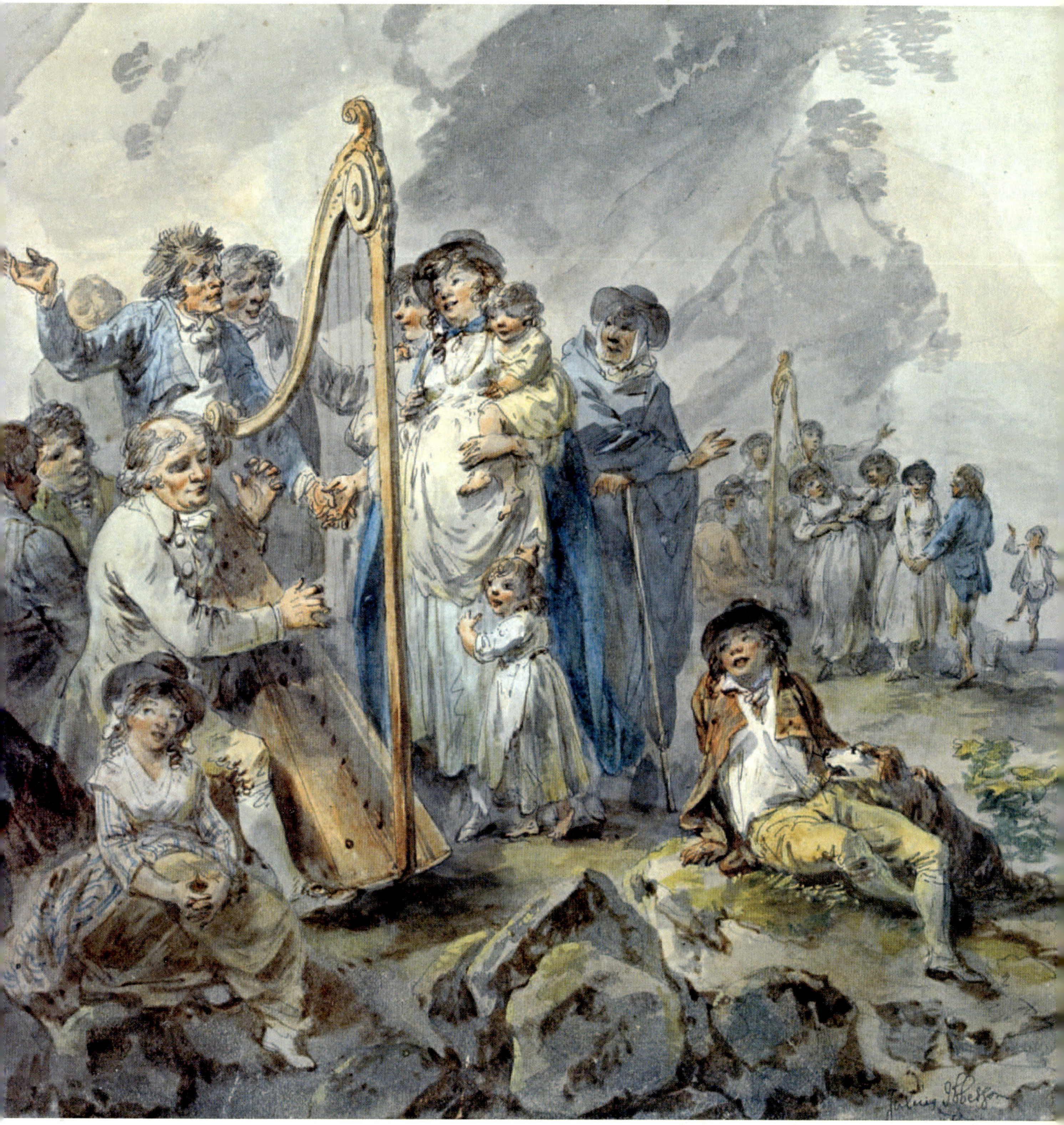

# American Glamour

## ELIZA RIDGLEY, 1818

*Thomas Sully*

Thomas Sully, an English born American artist, achieved fame and fortune as a portrait painter to the highest echelons of American society. Part of his success was through his ability to flatter the sitter, for he seemed to have no qualms about 'improving' the appearance of what he was painting. Certainly his most famous portrait in Britain (the Coronation painting of the 18-year-old Queen Victoria) is one of the most impressive of that long-reigning monarch, not particularly noted for her beauty.

*A harpist says:*

"For me, harp and harpist just don't seem to belong together."

In the picture opposite stands Eliza Ridgley, the 15-year-old daughter of a wealthy Baltimore merchant.

We can imagine that this portrayal of young Miss Ridgely, pausing during her rather casual tuning of the harp, wearing a revealing strapless dress and displaying a slender uncovered arm, might have been on the borderline of *risqué* in 1818. And although admiring the neoclassical design of the portrait and marvelling at the beauty of the satin costume, we might also wonder whether Eliza's arms were in reality *quite* so long or indeed whether she really played the harp at all? But as if to reassure the observer that the instrument is not just a prop, one of the pedals is depressed.

Although the harp itself (a French 'Louis XVI' instrument) seems to be rather plain, the power of the romanticism in this huge portrait is beyond doubt. Perhaps it is the instrument's understated features and straight soundboard and column which render it so suitable to act as a foil to the subject of the portrait?

Thomas Sully certainly hit the target with this one. It has achieved an iconic status as the finest American harpist portrait, and indeed has even been credited as an inspiration for the widespread American popularity of the instrument itself in the 19th century. It is impressively displayed in the National Gallery of Art, Washington DC.

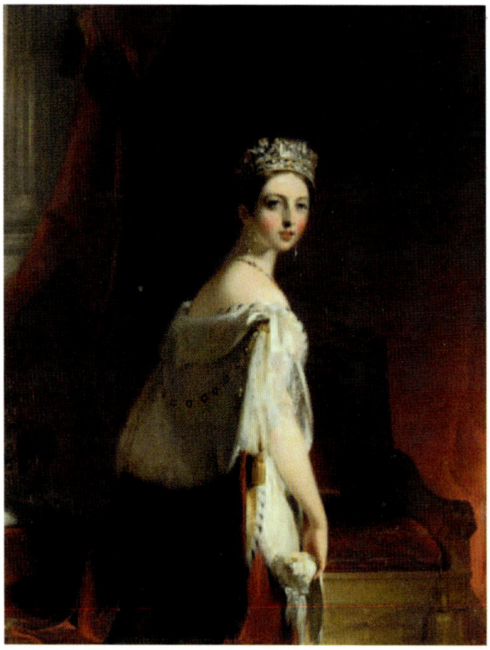

*Queen Victoria*
Thomas Sully, 1838

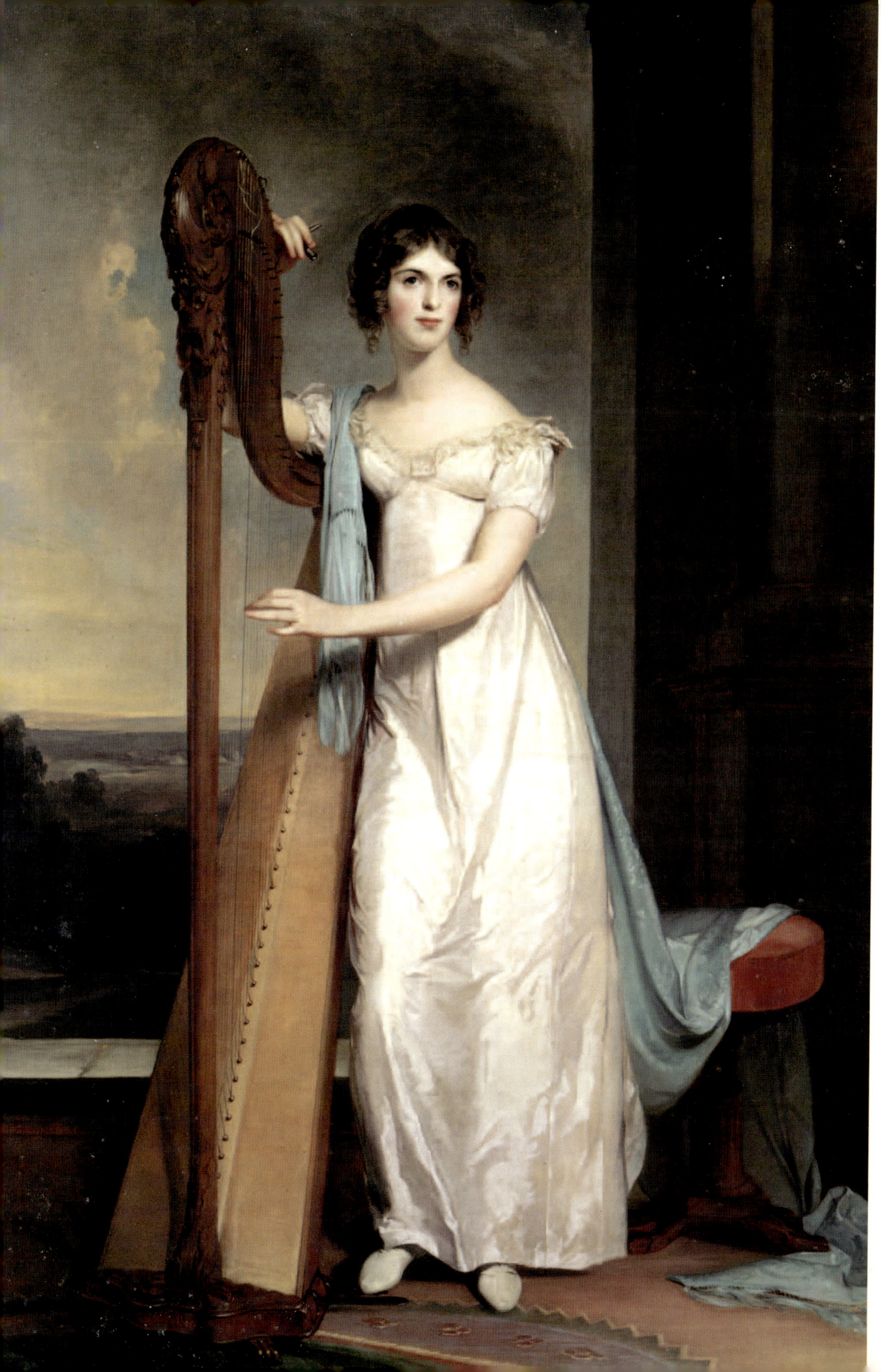

# Sir Walter Scott's Muse

## MARGARET, MARCHIONESS OF NORTHAMPTON, 1820

*Sir Henry Raeburn*

At first glance this appears to be just another nineteenth-century depiction of a young aristocratic lady playing the harp. It is that, but the lady concerned is one of the most interesting sitters in this collection.

*A harpist says:*

"She loves this harp. I can almost hear the music."

Born in 1791 in Torloisk on the island of Mull in the Scottish Hebrides, Margaret Douglas Maclain Clephane grew up to be a proficient linguist and classical scholar, collector of Gaelic melodies and a poet of distinction.[1] While still a teenager, she began a large collection of airs for the harp (together with a few for the guitar) with her sister Anna Jane. Many of these are traditional Scottish and Irish tunes, but there is also quite a cosmopolitan collection of music from other countries, France Italy, Portugal and Scandinavia included. A large number of the Gaelic melodies were collected or composed originally by the famous Irish harpist O'Carolan, but it seems likely that at least some were collected by Margaret or her sister.[2]

Margaret Clephane was the ward of Sir Walter Scott, the extraordinarily popular nineteenth-century poet and novelist and it was he who introduced her to her husband (later to become the 2nd Marquis of Northampton). Her relationship with the mighty Sir Walter appears to have been fulfilling and of mutual benefit. The times were those of a revival of interest in Scottish traditions and history and Margaret assisted the great writer with her personal knowledge of local legends and with translations from Gaelic, which she helped to teach him. He, in turn, was a father figure to her, assisting with her poetry and, negotiating a useful dowry and large allowance on her marriage to the future Marquis. It seems that Margaret was a significant influence on Scott's hugely successful novel *Waverley*[3] and a good case can be made that she was the inspiration for the character Flora McIvor. In one particularly theatrical moment in the novel Flora enchants her hero Waverley with her Gaelic speech and harp playing.[4]

Indeed it may well be that she is painted as Flora McIvor in this deeply romantic portrait by Raeburn. The nature of the harp is ambiguous; it may be a 'Caledonian harp' as mentioned in the novel; her Scottish shawl and dress and prominent Christian cross would certainly be more in keeping with the character of Flora than with that of an aristocratic lady in her Northampton-shire stately home.

Raeburn was the principal Scottish portraitist of the time, most famous for the iconic Scottish picture of a clergyman on ice (The Reverend Robert Walker Skating on Duddingston Loch)[5] and he is said to have completed more than 1000 portraits. The portrait of the *Marchioness of Northampton* is a fine example of his skill: he manages to capture the concentration and attitude of the 29-year old harpist 'in action' in a way only matched in this book by Hogarth, and the romantic drama of the picture is quite typical of his style. Although

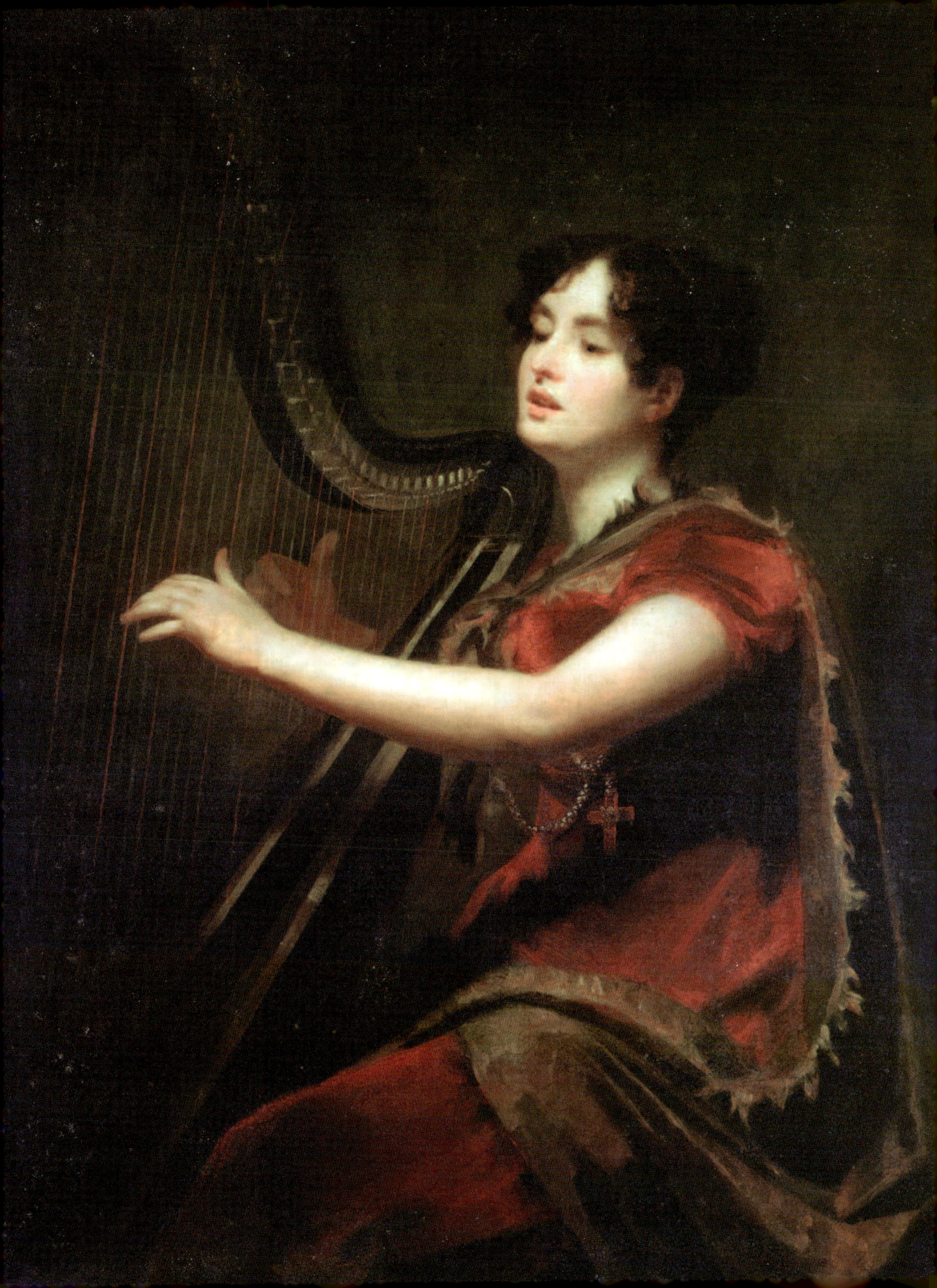

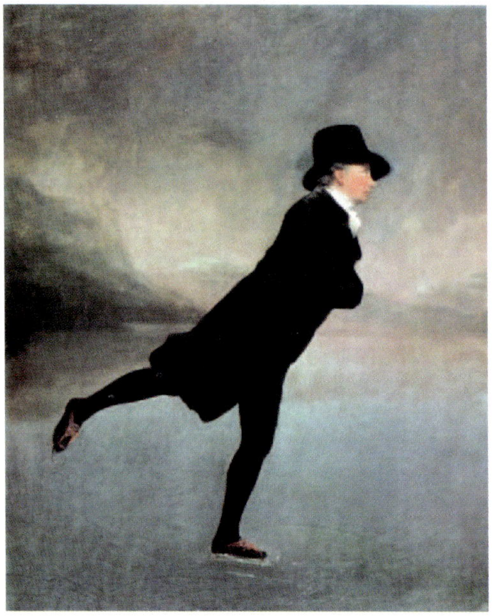

*Rev Robert Walker skating on Duddingston Loch*
Sir Henry Raeburn, 1784

much of the harp cannot be seen, his representation of the instrument is very careful, and the colouring and lighting of the portrait, in particular of the harpist's face, are almost photographic.

Margaret was happily married to Spencer Compton, cousin of the Prime Minister Spencer Perceval and, following his assassination, his successor as Member of Parliament. Shortly after Raeburn had painted portraits of her husband and herself the couple set off for an extended 'Grand Tour' to Italy lasting nearly 10 years. With her deep interest in and knowledge of classical culture and languages this must have been a fascinating time for Margaret. Tragically she died in childbirth in Italy in 1830.

Her poetry was not published in her lifetime, but was printed posthumously in 1833. Here is just one sample verse from her long narrative poem *Irene* which has a beautiful sensuous rhythm and one might almost say a musical resonance.

**LXXVIII.**

*How happy fled the hours! the slanting sun*
*Beyond the mountains set in floods of gold,*
*Ere the short course of day seem'd well begun.*
*Thus when light barks along the billows hold*
*Their course, and winds so soft their wings unfold*
*That scarce we feel their motion - the far shore*
*Seems flying from our sight - the outlines bold*
*Fade in the sky, and then are seen no more,*
*'Till the good port is hail'd, the unconscious voyage o'er.*

---

[1] It should not be assumed that Margaret Clephane grew up in an exceptionally wild or isolated area. Mull, always one of the most accessible of the Hebridean islands was then quite a thriving community. At the turn of the eighteenth and nineteenth centuries its population was approaching 10,000 – nearly five times what it is now.

[2] There is a copy in the National Library of Scotland. [The Maclean Clephane Collection: MS.14949]

[3] The novel was literally an overnight success in 1814 and was rapidly reprinted and translated. Following its publication Jane Austen wrote: 'Walter Scott has no business to write novels, especially good ones. -- It is not fair.' Berlioz's concert overture *Waverley* was completed in 1827. Edinburgh's principal railway station was named after the hero in 1854.

[4] 'I have given you the trouble of walking to this spot, Captain Waverley, both because I thought the scenery would interest you, and because a Highland song would suffer still more from my imperfect translation, were I to introduce it without its own wild and appropriate accompaniments. To speak in the poetical language of my country, the seat of the Celtic muse is in the mist of the secret and solitary hill, and her voice in the murmur of the mountain stream. He who wooes her must love the barren rock more than the fertile valley, and the solitude of the desert better than the festivity of the hall.'

Few could have heard this lovely woman make this declaration, with a voice where harmony was exalted by pathos, without exclaiming that the muse whom she invoked could never find a more appropriate representative. But Waverley, though the thought rushed on his mind, found no courage to utter it. Indeed, the wild feeling of romantic delight with which he heard the first few notes she drew from her instrument, amounted almost to a sense of pain.

He would not for worlds have quitted his place by her side; yet he almost longed for solitude, that he might decipher and examine at leisure the complication of emotions which now agitated his bosom.' *Waverley* by Sir Walter Scott , *Chapter XXII, Highland Minstrelsy* 1814.

5 Raeburn's authorship of this painting has recently been disputed.

# The Royal Mistress

## LADY ELIZABETH CONYNGHAM, 1822

*Sir Thomas Lawrence*

'Simpering on a sofa' was the derogatory description that Thackeray's upwardly aspiring character Becky Sharp applied to the most famous contemporary portrait of King George IV in the novel *Vanity Fair*.[1] Dressed not in regal finery but in a gentleman's clothes, and indeed, 'on a sofa', this royal portrait was painted by Sir Thomas Lawrence especially for the Marchioness Conyngham. No doubt Lady Elizabeth would have particularly appreciated this less formal portrayal of her lover, off-duty and bereft of his monarchical robes.

*A harpist says:*

"Beautiful harp. Beautiful harpist."

In return, the King's favourite portraitist would have taken particular pleasure in completing this splendid likeness of the royal mistress in his finest bravura style.

Beautifully bejewelled and attired, the Marchioness is seen in the picture opposite tuning not a conventionally grand full-size harp, but a rather small green Irish-style instrument. As with four of the final five portraits of ladies in this book, the harpist is in the act of tuning, but here the harpist is seated and the instrument's curves and decorations seem to complement rather than act as a foil for the sitter.

Lawrence's female portraits can be criticised as stylised. Be that as it may, that of Marchioness Conyngham must count as one of his very finest. Indeed, its inclusion by Walther in his series of *Masterpieces of Western Art* underlines its position as one of the classic portraits of the age.

The sitter's face, gazing slightly sideways into the eyes of the viewer, may indeed seem to be rather trapped in a Regency stereotype, but this portrait is alive with movement and colour. Take a look at the dress with its folds and graded transparency and, perhaps of particular interest to the present reader, the beautifully drawn harp. In an external setting with classical references, and superficially in the manner of a Gainsborough portrait, the

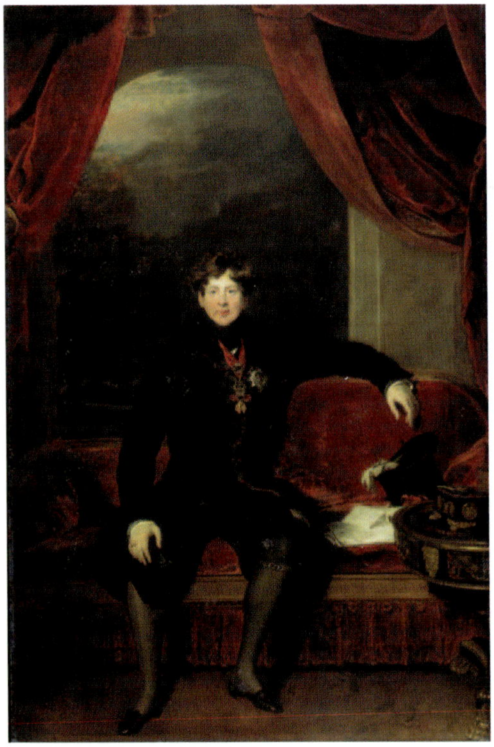

*George IV*
Sir Thomas Lawrence, 1822

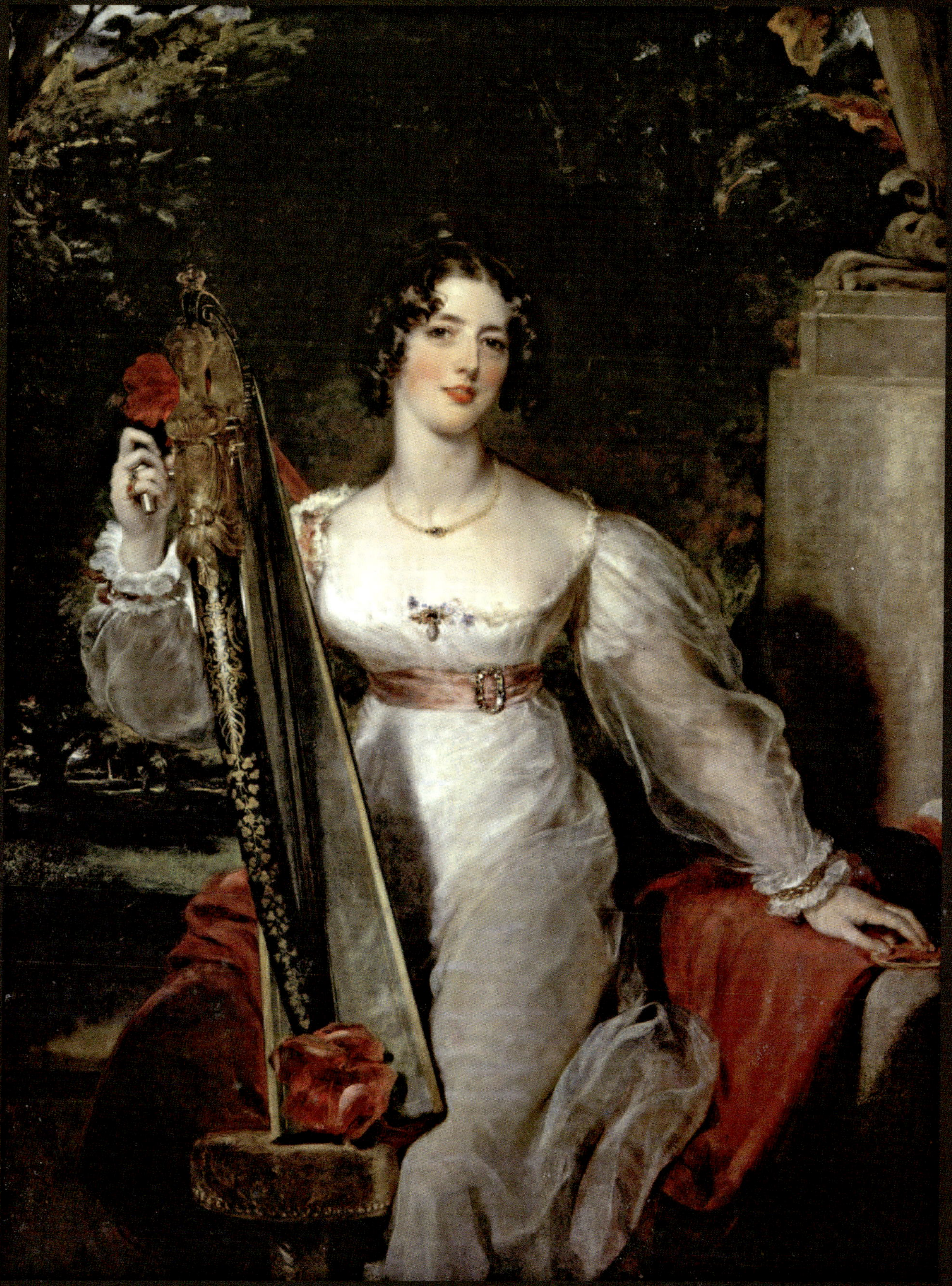

landscape here is of much less significance than it often might be with the earlier master, and it is the sitter herself who completely dominates the picture.

The green harp is known appropriately as an Egan 'Royal' It is most carefully painted with detailed decoration on the pillar, and this one is appropriately complete with a crown atop the carrying handle. In Lawrence's portrait, the head on whom the miniature crown is placed looks similar to that of George IV!

The Conynghams were of Irish aristocracy, (their estate was and is at Slane less than 30 miles from Dublin), and George IV stayed there when he visited Ireland in 1821. John Egan was the fashionable Dublin-based harp manufacturer of the time. Are we seeing here an early example of product placement?

What may be the actual instrument portrayed is on display in *Museo dell'Arpa Victor Salvi* in Piasco, near Cuneo in northern Italy. Described as a 'dital' harp — one with a manually operated mechanism — the museum commentary explains that in mechanical design it is similar to a miniature Erard pedal harp. The function of the pedals in altering the pitch of the strings is taken over by hand-operated ditals in the harp column which can clearly be seen in the photograph of the actual instrument below. Egan was an important manufacturer of forerunners of the modern Irish harp, and another rather less elaborate instrument by that maker is in the Victoria and Albert Museum, London.

Like Hogarth, Lawrence had been born the son of a poor innkeeper, and also like his predecessor, he was to spend much time in later life in theatrical circles.

Thomas Lawrence *père* was, in fact, the landlord of the celebrated 'American Coffee Shop' in Bristol, but sadly he was about 200 years too early in anticipating the fashion for such places of refreshment, and the enterprise foundered. The family decamped to the Black Bear Inn in Devizes, where the young Thomas (like the young Wolfgang Mozart) was set to work by his father, in his case by reciting and sketching travellers en route for society's favourite watering hole of Bath. Young Thomas's sisters had to provide the musical entertainment for the guests. Notable visitors included Queen Charlotte, the diarist Fanny Burney (daughter of the music historian Charles Burney), the actor Garrick, and, in a particularly fortunate encounter, a certain Daines Barrington.

Youthful talent was one of the many interests of Daines Barrington. He had publicised the prodigious abilities of the eight-year-old Wolfgang Amadeus Mozart on his visit to London in 1764. Thomas's remarkable flair for drawing was duly reported on by Barrington following his visit to Devizes.

After several years in nearby Bath, honing his craft and ingratiating himself to the rich, powerful and beautiful (including the actress Mrs Siddons and Georgiana, Duchess of Devonshire), Thomas moved onwards and upwards to London, where he rapidly attracted attention by submitting no less than seven pictures for the Royal Academy's wildly popular summer exhibition in 1787.

While in London he caught the attention of George III and the Prince Regent. When the latter ascended to the throne as George IV, royal patronage, along with the artist's technical mastery and impeccable manners, assured him the leading place as portraitist in England. Following Napoleon's final defeat at Waterloo the king dispatched Lawrence to paint all the leaders of the victorious allies. This resulted in a splendid series of portraits for the Waterloo Chamber in Windsor castle. Mainly as a result of this he became, along with Ingres and Goya, one of the most sought-after portraitists in the whole of western Europe. Quite an accomplishment for an innkeeper's son from the West Country.

This portrait of Lady Elizabeth Conyngham was part of the final long-lived flourish to Lawrence's career as a portraitist, an activity for him so prolific as to leave one to imagine that he believed the art form was going out of fashion. Which is, of course, exactly what it did.

Honoured by the nation on his death in 1830, Lawrence's demise was followed within weeks by that of his royal patron George IV. Society was quickly to forget the master portraitist and the *cognoscienti* of the art world turned their interest to the new and brilliant landscaping talents of Turner and Constable. Like many of Lawrence's works, the portrait of Lady Elizabeth Conyngham went abroad, where the artist's reputation was to some extent maintained.

The Marchioness now proudly greets visitors who enter the room of English paintings in the *Museu Calouste Gulbenkian* in Lisbon, where the portrait holds its own brilliantly alongside masterpieces by Gainsborough and Turner.

---

1 *Vanity Fair* by William Thackeray, 1847 chapter 48 'She went to Colnaghi's and ordered the finest portrait of him that art had produced, and credit could supply. She chose that famous one in which the best of monarchs is represented in a frock-coat with a fur collar, and breeches and silk stockings, simpering on a sofa from under his curly brown wig.'

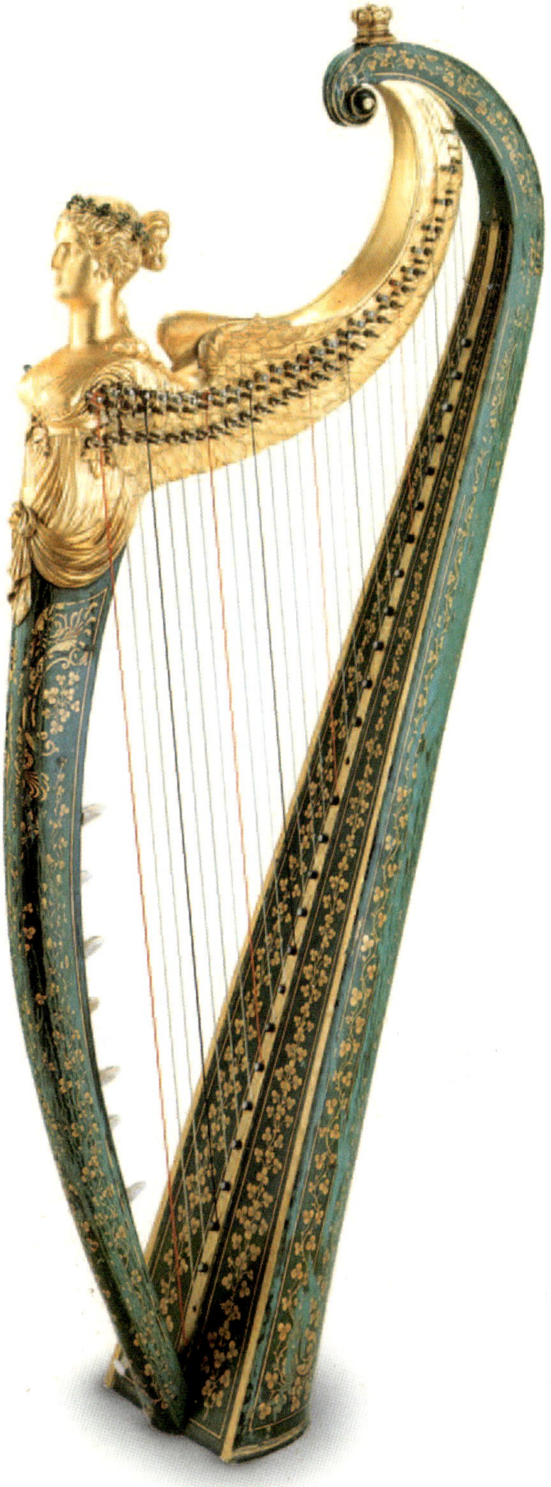

*Dital Harp*
by Egan and Sons, Dublin, c1820

# Exiled from France

## JULIETTE DE VILLENEUVE, 1824

*Jacques-Louis David*

This huge and magnificent portrait was little known and had never been reproduced until 1997 when it was acquired by the Louvre museum from the sitter's family. As the last large original painting by David, and a rare full-length portrait by the master (completed when the artist was 77 years old while in exile in Brussels), it has been instrumental in cementing the status of the work that he was doing towards the end of his life.

*A harpist says:*

"Nothing seductive here, but it's an immaculate harp with an immaculately presented harpist."

Always a political figure as well as an artist, Jacques-Louis David had been a prominent supporter of, and propagandist for the French Revolution of 1789. Unlike many artists, particularly those with aristocratic connections, he was able to stay on in France, even during the 'Terror' but later, tarred with the brush of association with the Committee of Public Safety he only narrowly avoided being executed alongside his friend Robespierre. When more peaceful times returned, he was released from prison, remarried his former wife (who had been sympathetic to the *ancien régime*) and, with an eye for the direction in which political power was shifting, requested a sitting with a certain general Napoleon. After the *coup d'état* of 1799, when his sitter became First Consul of France, he was commissioned to paint another picture of him, this time a propagandist depiction of his crossing of the Alps. He was then able to return to his career as a state sponsored painter of historical works, and portraitist of the front rank.

Following the battle of Waterloo and Napoleon's defeat and exile to St Helena, it seemed for a while that David might defy national sentiment, change his spots for a second time and join ranks with the restored Bourbon monarchy in Paris. Instead he decided to move to Brussels where he was able to spend time more congenially among exiled relatives and former associates of Napoleon.

Among them was Juliette de Villeneuve (1802–1840), closely connected to the Bonaparte family by two of her aunts and her own marriage. She was the host of a *salon* in Bruxelles frequented by David.

As in the earlier portraits by Ducreux and Sully, the harp is used as an impressive prop and foil for the sitter, and she is again in the act of tuning her instrument. The harp itself (an Erard 'Empire') is beautifully and realistically depicted with loose string ends and carefully painted details. The older master's hard-edged neoclassical lines and restrained tones seen here are in dramatic contrast to Lawrence's lush Regency colouring and Raeburn's deep romantic glimmering in nearly contemporary portraits earlier in this book.

In the Giroust triple portrait a number of objects of significance seem to have been deliberately positioned about the room. The

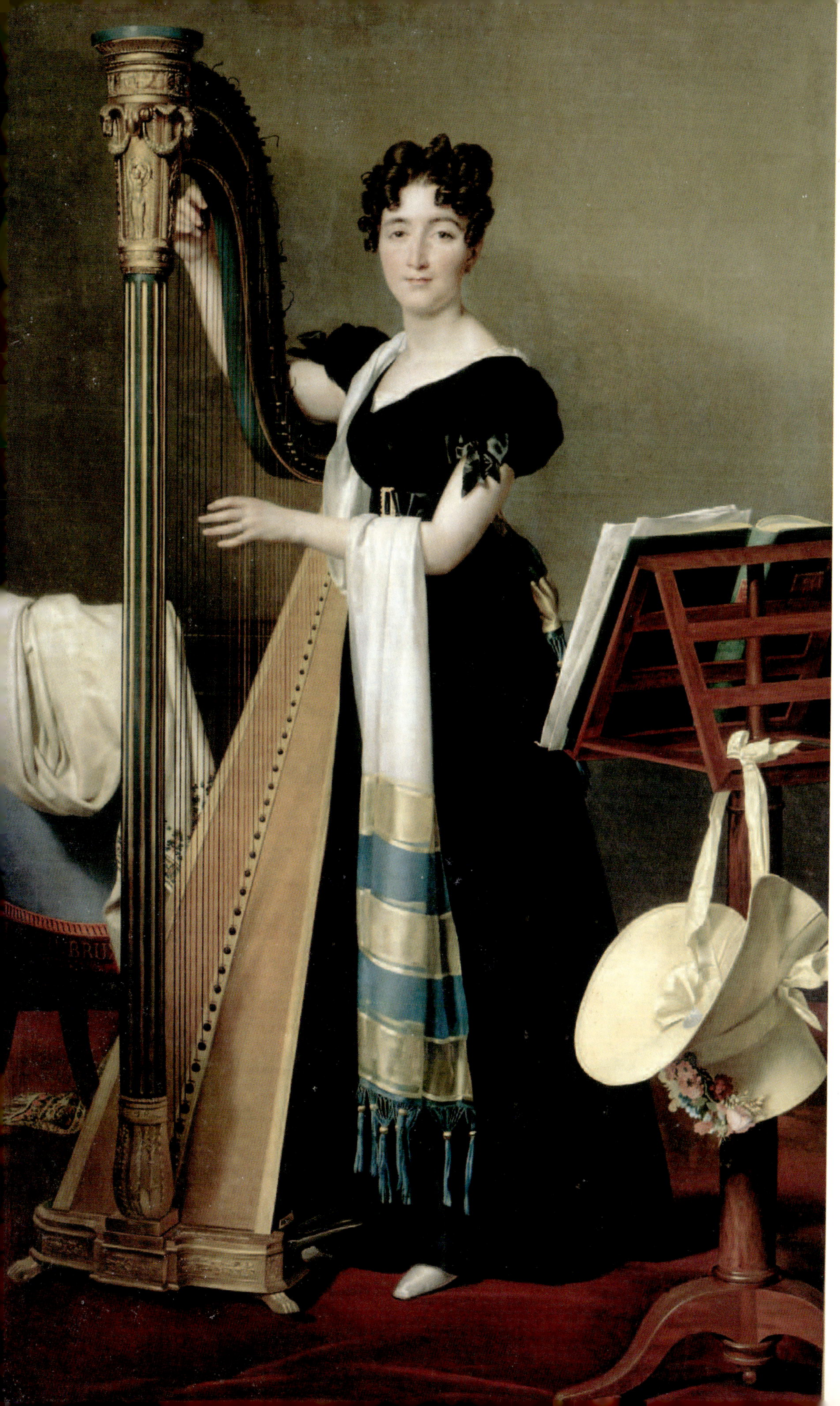
BRUX

same can be said of this portrait, but here there is little feeling for the room itself and the artefacts seem to have been artificially placed, as if in a still life. The legs of both the music stand and chair are cut off by the border of the painting, and in this, as with the dispassionate realism with which both the sitter and the props are depicted, David seems to be anticipating photography, 12 years before the actual event.

Fabrics are beautifully depicted: the elaborate straw hat and ribbon tying it to the music stand attract admiration, as does the shawl draped about the chair on the left and the particularly beautiful tasselled stole wrapped around Juliette's arm, over her shoulder, and just visibly down her back. Its slight sense of movement distinguishes it from the other objects in the picture, which seem to be frozen in time and space. David's skill at portraying colours and fabrics is seen in the sitter's dress, particularly the white edging at the top and the purple and gold on the buckle.

Jacques-Louis David is not generally credited for his perceptive psychology, but here the artist seems to capture perfectly the young woman's rather plain face: she addresses the viewer directly seeming rather more posed and less welcoming than Rose-Adélaïde Ducreux.

Although looking nostalgically backwards to an earlier era of neoclassic elegance, the portrait of Juliette de Villeneuve is in more senses than one a monumental work, of interest not only to harpists and musicians, but also to all lovers of early nineteenth-century art. As such it is a fitting conclusion to this series.

# Postscript

## THE VICTORIAN DRAWING ROOM

In 1837, just seven years after Lawrence's death, Victoria was on the throne. Genteel Regency Society was becoming a distant memory, and there had been an invention which was to ensure that the portrait was to lose its special place in the world of art – the photograph. With Daguerre's achievement in fixing a photographic image, the prized skill of the artist to capture an individual's likeness was compromised. The distinctiveness of this facet of the art form was lost and the painted portrait became just one genre among many.

The world of music changed too. With the inexorable rise of the piano, the harp faded from the dominance it once had in cultured society as the musical instrument for unmarried ladies. Erard's new fully chromatic harps with a 'double action' pedal mechanism, although more sonorous and suited to solo performance, were sometimes held to be too heavy and complex for young ladies to master, and perhaps not so well suited to the supposedly refined feminine character.

The instrument's primary focus shifted from the drawing room (and its American and French equivalents, the parlor and salon), to the concert hall, and the harp made its way into the romantic orchestra by way of composers such as Berlioz and Meyerbeer. A new generation of mainly foreign male harp showmen came to the fore. Bochsa, Dizi and Parish-Alvars now took to the stage alongside other composer-virtuosi such as Paganini, Chopin and Liszt.

However, the harp continued to be constructed as an instrument of supreme elegance, and it remained well suited to the feminine confines of the drawing room. This celebrated Victorian institution was the place where tea and music would be made, callers received and where ladies would withdraw to following dinner. It would customarily be adorned with works of art of appropriate respectability. Frequently portraits would be displayed, with ladies posing with a harp or sitting at the piano.

But the harpist portrait as a particular genre attracting the work of the finest masters of paint, simply faded away.

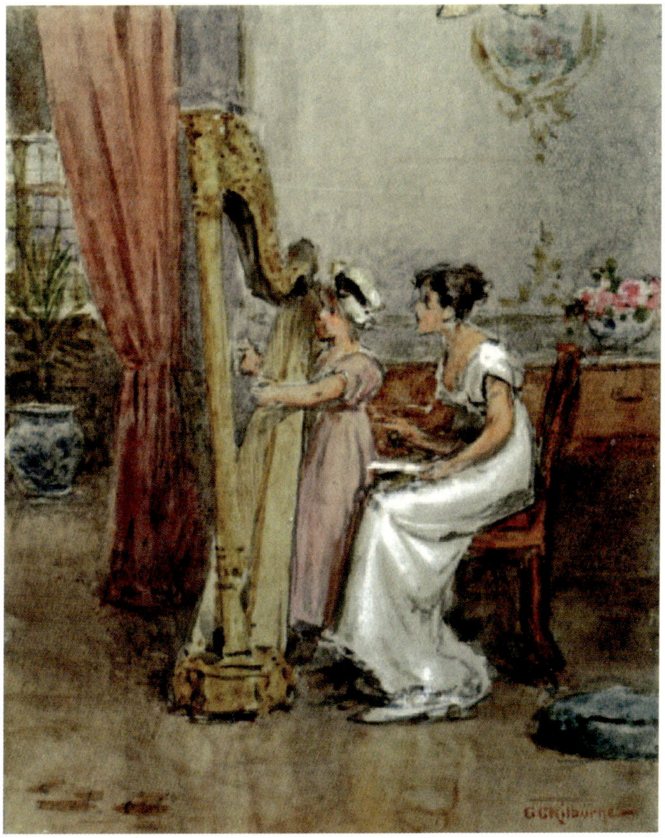

*The Harp Lesson*
George Kilburne, c1900

## Acknowledgements

The author is particularly indebted to the distinguished Dutch harpist and teacher Edward Witsenburg.

Grateful thanks are also due to the following: Lucy Coward, Martin J Holmes, Bill Hughes, Manon Hughes, Rebecca Millward, Ceinwen Roberts and Elin G Stuart

## References and further reading


| | | |
|---|---|---|
| **Battistini**, Matilde | 2002 | (English Edition 2005) *Symbols and Allegories in Art*, J Paul Getty Museum, Los Angeles |
| **Bénézit**, E | 1999 | *Dictionnaire des Peintres, Sculpteurs Dessinateurs et Graveurs*, Gründ, Paris |
| **Braun**, Martin | 2006 | 'The Greuze Mozart - rediscovery of a portrait painting' *web.telia.com/~u57013916/Greuze_Mozart_Braun.htm* |
| **Collings**, Matthew | 2003 | *Matt's Old Masters*, Weidenfeld & Nicolson, London |
| **Craske**, William | 2000 | *William Hogarth*, Tate Publishing, London |
| **Ellis**, Osian | 1980 | (reprinted 1991) *Hanes y Delyn yng Nghymru/The story of the Harp in Wales*, University of Wales Press, Cardiff |
| **Funnell**, Peter | 1992 | *The National Portrait Gallery at Bodelwyddan Castle*, The National Portrait Gallery, London |
| **Gombrich**, E H | 1972 | *The Story of Art*, Phaidon, Oxford |
| **Griffiths**, Ann | 1980 | 'Harp', *New Grove Dictionary of Music and Musicians*, 2nd edition, Oxford University Press |
| **Hess**, Dr Daniel | 2007 | *Bildnis des Johannes Xylotectus*, (article) Germanisches Nationalmuseum, Nuremburg |
| **Hockney**, David | 2006 | *Secret Knowledge*, Thames & Hudson, London |
| **Kitson**, Michael | 1966 | *The Age of Baroque*, Paul Hamlyn, London |
| **Levy**, Michael | 2005 | *Sir Thomas Lawrence*, Yale University Press. New Haven & London |
| **Marson**, John | 2005 | *The Book of the Harp*, Kevin Mayhew Ltd, Stowmarket, Suffolk |
| **Mandell**, Laura | 2005 | *Scottish Women Poets of the Romantic Period*, University of Chicago |
| **Michel**, Régis | 1988 | *David, L'art et le politique*, Gallimard, Paris |
| **National Gallery of Art** | 1992 | *National Gallery of Art*, (catalogue)Thames & Hudson, New York |
| **Rensch**, Roslyn | 1969 | *The Harp, Its History, Technique and Repertoire*, Duckworth, London |
| **Rimmer**, Joan | 1965 | The Morphology of the Triple Harp, *Galpin Society Journal*, March 1965 |
| **Rimmer**, Joan (et al.) | 2002 | Grove Music online, Harp, Macmillan Publishers Ltd <*http://www.grovemusic.com*> |
| **Rosser**, Ann | 1981 | *Telyn a Thelynor*, Amgueddfa Genedlaethol Cymru, Cardiff |
| **Royal Academy of Arts** | 2006 | *Citizens and Kings, Portraits in the age of revolution 1760 –1830* London & Paris |
| **Sampaio**, Luísa | 2004 | Articles in *Calouste Gulbenkian Museum Guide*, Lisbon |
| **Simon**, Robin | 2007 | *Hogarth, France and British Art*, Hogarth Arts, London |
| **Sumner**, Ann | 1988 | Gainsborough's 'Portrait of Lady Clarges', *The Burlington Magazine*, Vol. 130, No. 1027 (Oct. 1988) pp. 761-763 |
| **Vandervellen**, Pascalle | 2000 | *Plucked Stringed Instruments*, (No 4 of series) Musée des Instruments de Musique, Bruxelles |
| **Walther**, Ingo (Editor) | 2002 | *900 Masterpieces of Western Art*, Taschen GmbH, Cologne |
| **West**, Shearer | 2004 | *Portraiture*, Oxford History of Art, OUP, Oxford |
| **Wilkins**, David G | 2005 | *Big Book of Art*, Collins, London |
| **Witzenmann**, Wolfgang | 2004 | 'Marco Marazzoli', *New Grove Dictionary of Music and Musicians*, 2nd edition, Oxford University Press |